Cognitive Behavioral Therapy

The Ultimate Guide to Defeat Anxiety, Depression, Anger, Panic Attacks and Negative Thoughts to Improve your Mental Health and Regain Control of Your Life

Table of Contents

Introduction

With a growing passion for cognitive-behavioral therapies, I have written this book to support patients with their day-to-day practices and use such strategies. I have attempted to write it in a concise and realistic manner, explain basic approaches for the execution of cognitive-behavioral treatments, address theoretically challenging strategies, and recommend possible solutions to these issues.

Cognitive-behavioral therapy is a standardized, time-limited therapeutic technique focused on research aimed at solving the emotional issues of patients. The therapy focuses on problems and is goal-oriented, in that issues are specifically defined and concrete strategies are decided to resolve the defined problems. Problems and goals are generally defined in terms of emotions, patterns, behavior and the day-to-day activity of the patient. Both facets of therapy are adequately defined and the therapist and patient work together in a timely manner with various approaches.

According to Twaddle and Blackburn, CBT's main components include mutual psychological understanding of the present issues of the patient in a clinical sense; positive communication between patients and physicians including a complete sharing of knowledge; a questioning style that assists patient comprehension (this is also known as Socratic questioning in the cognitive-behavioral therapy literature); and acquiring knowledge from experience especially that which takes place outside the session.

As other therapeutic treatments, in the area of cognitive-behavioral therapy, there is reasonable discussion as to where treatment should be focused. The importance of cognitive-behavioral therapy, the importance of interpersonal interaction, and the suitability of the patient's disposition for cognitive-behavioral treatments are some of the topics addressed in everyday practice. To some degree, the way practitioners deal with this subject reflects the cognitive-behavioral therapy training they received and the CBT physicians, coaches and managers whose theoretical experiences and professional skills have impacted their training.

The cognitive-behavioral therapy research demonstrates these variations in emphasis, with distinction made between cognitive and behavioral therapies. Using the concept of agoraphobia and panic disorder as an example, the original approach tackled avoidant behavior, which was reinforced by the theory of conditioning and the therapy rationale based on the idea of graded stimulus exposure designed to lead to habituation. Clark's paradigm (1986) focuses on cognition and stresses behavioral experiments for evaluating if the patient panic-related cognitions to panic symptoms is right. In the meantime, Barlow (1993) proposed a synthesis of these two statements but emphasized a more theoretical position on behavior. There is good evidence that the two models have been successful in clinical trials, but deciding the model to use may be challenging. Clinicians in the preparation process always follow the strategies they were taught.

For both beginners and seasoned cognitive-behavioral therapy professionals, though, these problems may cause difficulties and dilemmas that must be addressed by each clinician herself in a realistic manner. This resolve requires knowledge and realistic experience in using CBT, and I will urge readers to address the problems with their peers, CBT coaches and CBT medical supervisors as an first step in exploring your own personal viewpoints on these topics. What I will expect you to do in this pursuit is to stay faithful to the spirit of CBT's scientific-practice model. This approach is based on the concept of the individual professional investigating, questioning , and assessing on a regular basis in order to create reliable and successful treatment techniques.

In an attempt to recognize these differences, the book attempts to lay the foundations for some core cognitive-behavioral therapy principles. The development of cognitive-behavioral therapy assessment skills and basic concepts for the sensation of psychological issues in a CBT framework are strongly emphasized. I will also spend time trying to help the patient to concisely define their present problems and to define objectives in connection with these problems. The significance of the therapeutic relationship in the theoretical framework of CBT would be emphasized. The user is urged to establish a clear understanding of the scope of evidence supporting cognitive-behavioral therapy interventions and to use it as a guide for making their own decisions on the use of cognitive-behavioral therapy interventions for individual clients. The reader is also advised to take a careful look at the evidence base and acknowledge that some of the proof is incomplete. New treatments are evolving, and practitioners need to develop their theoretical awareness and clinical skills appropriately through ongoing studies into the efficacy of CBT. It should also be remembered that cognitive-behavioral therapy is not ideal for all issues and all patients.

Following Padesky and Greenberger (1995), the authors should conclude at the theoretical level that interventions should take place in one of five fields: feelings, physical sensations, environment, thoughts, and behavior. The work of Padesky is predicated on the Beckian CBT model, which theoretically forms the basis of this book.

An assessment, method, goals, and evidence-based procedure is the basis for intervention in the five fields of clinical judgment. An 'ideal' cognitive-behavioral therapy treatment

will lead to profound and lasting transformations in patients'
perceptions and beliefs associated with longer-term behavioral,
cognitive, physical and environmental improvements. For
various reasons, this certainly is not always the situation for
every patient. These can include pragmatic reasons such as the
patient's wishes, the resources available to treat him and the
physician's level of experience. Furthermore, the existing
shortcomings of cognitive-behavioral therapy theory and
approaches should be taken into account to tackle mental
health issues.

In an attempt to recognize these differences, the book attempts
to lay the foundations for some core CBT principles. The
production of CBT assessment skills and basic concepts for the
sensation of psychological issues in a CBT system are strongly
emphasized. I will spend time helping the patient to concisely
define their existing problems and to define objectives in
connection with them. The significance of the therapeutic
relationship in the theoretical framework of CBT would be
emphasized. The reader should gain a clear understanding of
the basis of evidence supporting CBT interventions and use that
as a basis for decision-making in the particular patients about
which CBT interventions should be used. The reader is also
advised to take a careful look at the evidence base and agree that
some of the information is inconclusive. New approaches are
evolving, and clinicians need to develop their theoretical
awareness and clinical skills appropriately through ongoing

studies into the efficacy of CBT. It should also be remembered that CBT is not ideal for all issues and all patients.

Following Padesky and Greenberger (1995), I acknowledge at the logical level that interventions should take place in one of five fields: the environment, physical sensations, feelings, thoughts, and behavior. The work of Padesky is based on the Beckian CBT model, which theoretically forms the basis for this book.

A clinical assessment, the formulation, the objectives, and evidence-based procedure is used for intervention in the five fields. An 'ideal' CBT protocol will lead to profound and lasting adjustments in patients' perceptions and beliefs associated with longer-term behavioral, cognitive, physical and environmental improvements. For different reasons, this is clearly not always the case with every patient. These can include pragmatic reasons such as the patient's wishes, the resources available to treat him and the clinician's level of experience. Furthermore, the existing shortcomings of CBT theory and approaches should be taken into account to tackle mental health issues.

CBT treatments have been shown to be successful with a diverse range of disorders. For instance, there is now proof of different effectiveness levels in obsessive-compulsive disorder, post-traumatic stress disorder, eating disorders, generalized anxiety, social phobia, bulimia nervosa, sexual addiction, specific phobia, acute and chronic depression, panic attack with and without agoraphobia, drugs, and alcohol among other illnesses.

The degree that can be anticipated with each disorder is the strength of evidence for these disorders and the extent of recovery. These are very important in deciding whether CBT interventions should be used and must be considered before they begin to be used. It is also useful to differentiate between using CBT procedures to address a specific problem and using the intervention to manage the chronic problem more effectively.

This book intends to introduce you to both CBT theory and CBT practice so that you can begin to use this valuable tool in your own life. The following chapters will enable you to:

- Appreciate some of the peculiar characteristics of the cognitive-behavioral approach.
- Get acquainted with the basic principles, processes, and models of CBT.
- Learn how to organize your own challenges within the context offered by CBT.
- Find helpless thinking and behavior patterns which can contribute to your difficulties.
- Build concrete step-by-step approaches to resolve the issues using proven principles in cognitive-behavioral techniques.

I hope this book will be informative and helpful, as with the books I've read myself. According to the CBT treatment style, you should spend some time reflecting on the content of each chapter when you have successfully completed reading it and, in particular, finish up the practice I included. It is tempting to skip these exercises, but if you can just invest a little time doing them, they will improve your understanding and help you associate the text with your own study.

Chapter 1 - Brief Cognitive-Behavioral Therapy

Over the past 50 years, CBTs have become effective mainstream psychosocial treatment options for many behavioral and emotional troubles. Behavior therapy methods were first formulated in the 1950s when experimentally based behavior standards were implemented to change the maladaptive human behavior. The 1970s also saw cognitive processes as an important field of psychological distress (Bandura, 1969). This led to the development and eventual integration of cognitive-therapy techniques and behavioral methodologies to form cognitive-behavioral therapies for different psychological disorders. In this report, we discuss the evidence of short forms of CBT in different disorders. First, we take into account the fundamental principles of CBT, which make such therapies suitable for abbreviated formats.

Basic Premises Of CBT

While several different cognitive-behavioral approaches have been developed to solve a variety of certain health conditions, all these strategies are underlying a collection of basic concepts and assumptions. In the first place, psychological dysfunction is understood by learning and processing mechanisms. The fundamental theory of learning incorporates the findings on classical and operational conditioning from laboratory research. For example, some phobic symptoms may be a classically conditioned fear reaction which continues long after the original unconditional stimulus has been removed. In this case, repeated, unreinforced exposure to the affected stimuli is presumed to eradicate the conditioned fear response. In a similar way, operant conditioning describes how unpleasant symptoms or habits are preserved in conjunction with the following consequences. For example, chronic pain behavior is thought to be largely maintained by attention from others. Therapies designed by early operant conditioning research that teach people to operate in their environment to enhance positive reinforcement for adaptive behavior, and reduce reinforcement in problematic behavior. Cognitive work indicates that inconsistencies in the perception of self-knowledge and environmental knowledge are central to many behavioral and psychological issues. For instance, bias in addressing data threats or interpreting unclear situations as threats contributes to unneeded or excessive anxiety. Similarly, memory problems or negative event information may lead to a depressed mood. The cognitive therapies are based on learning to change evaluations, core belief, and associated attention and memory biases.

Second, the treatment approach for cognitive-behavioral is guided by an experimental orientation towards human behavior, where each behavior is seen to depend on the particular environmental and internal conditions around it. This allows behavior to be understood and predicted better once its purpose is disclosed. Given that both cognitive and overt behavior are seen as adaptive and subject to adjustment, the cognitive environment is as well suitable for therapeutic treatment. Thus, CBTs are designed to address particular symptoms and behaviors described in the diagnosis or that present a treatment issue. The cognitive-behavioral practitioner approaches therapy under the premise that the symptoms and behavioral patterns observed are responsible for a certain fundamental or core feature (i.e., legal partnerships occur between this core component and the maladaptive symptoms that arise). Therefore, as soon as the main feature is recognized, handled and changed, the resultant maladaptive feelings, symptoms, and behavior will as well change. For instance, a panic disorder CBT therapist can discover that the patient has the mistaken impression that quick heartbeat implies a heart attack. Treatment would thus challenge this belief with cognitive restructuring and education, while at the same time motivating the patient to experience the sense of a quick heartbeat intentionally in order to know that a heart attack does not take place.

Thirdly, change is driven by new learning experiences that

overpower previous types of information processing and maladaptive learning. For example, confronting objects or circumstances that are feared without retreat or avoidance would allow new strategies and safety decisions to be made. Therefore changes can occur in the short term as a consequence of learning these new ideas and conduct and will be retained in the long term as these recently gained responses generalize across time and situations. CBT often includes the teaching of new coping skills (such as relaxation, assertiveness, or self-talk) for better environmental responses. This is supposed to lead to better results over time as new competencies or skills are performed and implemented repeatedly. Therefore, clinical improvement can occur in two separate pathways. First, because previous maladaptive behaviors and thoughts are substituted by more adaptive responses, new learning is created by new experiences. Secondly, the person can learn impactful coping abilities that lead to an enhanced functioning over time, as these abilities are repeatedly performed and developed.

Fourthly, the importance of the scientific approach for CBT expressed in the therapist's continuous measurement of change in the individual patient level. CBT therapists come up with hypotheses about the cognitive and behavioral patterns of an individual from their experimental orientation, take action according to that hypothesis, examine the resulting behavior, and adjust their hypothesis on the grounds of this observation, etc. The CBT therapist, therefore, is not simply tied to a series of techniques, but to practices in a fundamental and scientifically consistent philosophical stance (Goldfried & Davison 1994). The vast number of randomly generated, controlled psychotherapy outcome studies on CBT effectiveness also reflect this experimental approach. In 1995, a task force in the Clinical Psychology Division of the American Psychological Association analyzed the literature on psychotherapy outcomes in order to decide which interventions were deemed successful based on certain scientific parameters. By their 1996 update, 22 different therapies have been considered "well-established," meeting the most rigorous effectiveness testing requirements while a further 25 therapies have met the less rigorous requirements "probably effective therapy." The vast majority of these "empirically supported treatments" were cognitive-behavioral treatments for various conditions, including eating disorders, substance abuse, physical health problems, anxiety disorders, depression, and marital problems. There is therefore plenty of research evidence supporting the use of CBT to treat a number of clearly defined symptoms and behavioral disorders.

CBT is tailored to brief formats through the cognitive-behavioral conceptualization of psychological distress, the basic essence of the CBT goal, the proposed therapeutic improvement mechanisms, and the validity of the scientific method. This means that, until the basic maladaptive behavior and information processing is known, basic therapeutic behavior environments can be organized and the ability to cope can be taught in a very short time. Similarly, a continuous efficacy assessment of CBT allows the analysis of variations in its delivery. One of such variation is the treatment length.

CBT therapies are usually brief and time-limited as a consequence of the problem-focused approach. Many CBT therapies lead to major clinical changes and elimination of symptoms in just 10–20 sessions as opposed to other types of psychotherapy. But treatment researchers are now seeking to optimize current, cost-effective, and easily accessible CBTs. Some approaches to improving the efficacy of CBT interventions include the transfer of individual counseling to a group environment, self-help material and bibliotherapy and computer therapy programs. However, the most common solution to change in quality is to reduce the number of treatment sessions by shortening the number of current CBT treatments. This pattern not only represents a realistic answer to external pressures such as the emergence of controlled healthcare in the USA but also demonstrates the simple belief that successful CBT results from recognizing and modifying particular cognitions and attitudes, which are responsible for the problem. As research into CBT therapy advances, more effective therapies are developed that only involve interventions that lead to meaningful changes. Likewise, when more evidence points to the possible cause of a specific condition, therapies are best aimed at the maladaptive feature in need of intervention.

Brevity has a range of obvious benefits. Increased cost-efficiency could make healthcare available for more people. Patients experience rapid therapy benefits, which can also boost therapy reputation and increase the incentive for more improvements. However, in some cases, this strategy can be disadvantageous. CBT approach presumes that the change target is specifically defined and limited. More lengthy treatment may be needed for patients with more diffuse symptoms or with special comorbid situations, who interfere with targeted programs (including Axis II diseases). The abbreviated approach as well presumes that the patient is inspired and willing to make behavioral and cognitive change. Patients who are completely indifferent about change and are unwilling to fulfill the required homework assignments may therefore not receive treatments with very limited time frames. Likewise, brief CBT puts a greater pressure on the patient to be involved in both sessions. The CBT patient bears tremendous responsibility for learning the required therapeutic material and execution of relevant exercises, considerably more so when such treatment is shortened. Finally, the short CBT approach allows the therapist to be able to concentrate the patient on the particular therapy goals and activities. This allows the therapist to guide patients effectively and maintain a good therapeutic relationship. Not all therapists may be tailored for brief CBT. These prospective drawbacks evidently require empirical investigation.

Characteristics of Cognitive Behavioral Therapy

Basically, cognitive-behavioral therapy has the following characteristics:

<u>Based on the cognitive model of responses connected with emotions</u>: Cognitive-behavioral therapy is focused not on external factors, such as individuals, events or situations, but on changing people's thoughts and feelings. This allows the person to function and feel better, even if things don't change.

<u>It is rapid</u>: The most rapid form of therapy intended for treating psychological disorders is the cognitive behavioral therapy. Formal treatment ends if both the client and the therapist are content with the improvement that has been demonstrated and the client is able to deal with similar difficulties in the future.

<u>Developing a great therapeutic relation along with focused approach</u>: For adequate treatment, a positive relationship is required between the therapist and the client. Cognitive-behavioral therapists concentrate on empowering their clients with the opportunity to receive self-counseling skills and then the client may become self-sufficient. This can only take place if the client can be physically relaxed or comfortable with the therapist.

The efforts are collaborative: Cognitive-behavioral therapists strive to learn more about their client's emotions and thoughts. They try to assist them in achieving their life goals. The therapist's responsibility is to listen, understand and teach simultaneously, while the responsibility of the client is to express openly his or her worries, fears and to show willingness to absorb the therapist's lessons.

Cognitive behavioral therapy is an organized and directive approach towards treatment: Every cognitive behavioral therapy session has a clear agenda. The techniques shown to the client are matched with each of their objectives.

Cognitive behavioral therapy is based on model of induction: The inductive method is employed to enhance the differentiation of misconceptions and presumptions from reality and practical issues of life. This allows the person to accept the positive and to throw away the unreal negative thoughts that has been weighing him down.

Homework for clients: The clients are asked, during their counseling sessions, to incorporate the skills and strategies taught. The client can't overcome his problem without putting the skills and strategies into practice. Homework therefore becomes an unavoidable part of cognitive behavioral therapy.

Why Is CBT So Popular?

CBT has recently been very attractive. Its current success lies not only in their importance to a wide range of emotional problems, but as well in its "goodness of fit" for our times' values and priorities.

<u>It is accessible</u>: Sometimes referred to as "psychology of common sense." The cognitive-behavioral therapy is much simpler than the nuanced and sometimes counter-intuitive Freud and Jung theories. By figuring out how our ideas, emotions and behaviors affect one another, it is relatively straightforward to define priorities and methods for addressing all the problems you face with a little practice.

<u>It is skills-based</u>: Cognitive-behavioral therapies is deeply entrenched in an educational approach. Therapy does not suggest that a specialist 'fixes' you, but rather that you learn to overcome your own issues and to take care of your own mental health. One of the critics of conventional therapies is that consumers will rely on their therapist emotionally. Cognitive-behavioral therapies strongly discourages this dependency: the therapist is someone whose work is to facilitate and equip you, and this way of working is less threatening for a lot of people. However, the solution that is right for you must always be sought.

<u>It has a proven track record</u>: Cognitive-behavioral therapies is all about evidence, so it is not shocking that Beck and his supporters from the beginning were very stringent in estimating its effectiveness. CBT is undoubtedly studied more than most other types of therapy and is often targeted in a realistic, measurable way at identifying patient benefits. In the psychoanalytic tradition, this can be quite difficult to do. In this type of treatment improvement is so rooted in patient experience that it can be scientifically difficult to quantify. To make its current recommendations on which psychological therapies are the most suitable for different prominent psychological conditions, NICE centered its 2011 guidelines on a thorough analysis of existing clinical literature, most of which was reviewed by Anthony Roth and Peter Fonagy in the newest edition of their book.

<u>It can deliver rapid results</u>: One of the most significant selling points in CBT is the fairly quick mastery of the basic concepts. While conventional psychotherapy requires several years of weekly sessions, the majority of CBT courses are time-limited and seek to provide people with the skills they need within only a couple of months. In May 2012, there was a heartwarming study, which found that the suffering of children who have been victims of war in Central Africa has been decreased by more than 50 percent by just 15 CBT sessions. Because the outcomes are equivalent to other time-consuming treatments, it is understandable that the CBT treatment model fits in simply

with health systems juggling limited budgets. For example, for any person treated with CBT for schizophrenia, NICE guidelines reference possible net savings of £1000 per individual. Due to the fact that research frequently suggest a fairly brief CBT intervention to be also clinically successful, makes it very normal for health care professionals to believe that they are looking at a win-win scenario. This is why the UK administration spends millions in the growth of CBT services.

We present in the next chapters a summary of the scientific evidence supporting CBT practice. Although the "brief" CBT concept has no explicit, standard definition, we have found interventions requiring less than 10 sessions. The cutback was built on the observation that the new standard CBT treatments usually covers 10-20 sessions. We found empirical studies on the effectiveness of brief CBT by questioning experts in a wide variety of fields for available research and psychological abstract research. This section is not an exhaustive analysis of the existing literature, but instead a summary focusing on research designs that used randomized controlled group psychotherapy outcomes. Our review was structured according to diagnostic category, as the effectiveness of short CBT in different disorders was not empirically investigated.

Several issues have been noteworthy when reviewing the research for brief CBT to date. The first question that we have already responded to is that some disorders may be more susceptible to brief CBT than other disorders. In particular, more circumscribed illnesses, like specific phobias, with more readily quantifiable lawful relationships, tend to be best suited to short CBT. In agreement, the specific phobias have been researched more than almost any other disorder with respect to brief CBT. For example, how can the effectiveness of the short CBT be assessed? We found very few research specifically comparing abbreviated to unabbreviated CBT and those frequently "confused" by the use of supplementary self-help resources for abbreviated CBT alone. Unconfounded findings were discovered in the treatment of specific phobias alone. Most studies contrast brief CBTs with other forms of therapy (for example, non-directive), a placebo monitor, or a waiting list control. However, the relative advantages of brief CBT against unabbreviated CBT are not directly measured by such designs.

A third underlying problem concerns the parameters of abbreviated and unabbreviated CBT: does abbreviated CBT have as effective a long-term response, an acute response, and non-target symptoms and circumstances as non-abbreviated CBT? In most research, short-term, acute responses and long-term status are measured. Despite the concern that relapse can be raised after brief CBT with respect to unabbreviated CBT, especially if skills and new learning do not replicate and improve after the end of treatment, evidence generally indicates that the brief CBT has good long-term responses. Evidence of the advantages of unabbreviated CBT in relation to nontargeted signs and comorbid conditions is growing, at least for anxiety disorders. For instance, targeted therapies for panic disorders contribute to dramatic changes in other comorbid anxiety conditions, depressive disorders and Axis II attributes. Some studies have explored the impact of brief CBT on behavior not unique to the particular disease (e.g., general anxiety, depression, and psychological functioning), but the assessment also needs to be carried out as to whether brief CBT has the same general effect on reported comorbid conditions.

A fourth question is that the therapeutic improvement mechanism in brief CBT is the same as in unabbreviated CBT. Rachman & Whittal (1989) contrasted fast and slow responders for fear of spiders and snakes to exposure therapy. They believed that steady and gradual reductions in fear represent a sort of trial and error learning, while rapid decreases in fear reflect comprehension and reasoning, analogous to a "flashbulb." The goal of the brief CBT is, of course, to organize the learning interactions so that this second form of learning can be maximized. To date, therapeutic mechanisms have scarcely been researched.

One final question concerns individual differential variables estimating brief CBT outcomes such as severity, treatment attitudes, chronicity, and prolonged life stressors. Some available scientific study argues that positive attitudes towards treatment, as with standard CBT, predict a treatment response to brief CBT. Other findings indicate that brief CBT with less extreme populations can be more successful. However, several studies have found no major outcome predictors. More work is required to explain which characteristics contribute to improved outcomes of care under which conditions of care. Lastly, the relationship between therapeutic variables, such as experience levels and therapeutic outcomes is also important and has rarely been examined.

Panic Disorder And Agoraphobia

A variety of advances have been made to reduce the variety of panic disorder and agoraphobia therapy sessions. Traditional CBT is delivered in 10-20 sessions with a number of treatment components (Craske, 1999). Education and perceptual development tackle myths and misunderstandings of the nature of bodily sensations. Even corrective breathing strategies are used to control breathing. Ultimately, various types of in vivo exposure and interceptive are intended to minimize anxiety and to avoid agoraphobic conditions and physical sensations. Several studies support the use of abbreviated CBT to treat agoraphobia and panic disorder.

One series of experiments compared short clinical CBT approaches to self-help therapy. Lindren et al. (1994) observed a significant decrease of fear and agoraphobia symptoms for a variety of result measures in eight-session CBT therapy groups relative to a waiting list situation. They also found that eight-week, self-help care with bibliotherapy was similarly successful. In a later study, the research group observed that an eight-session self-administered bibliography therapy comprising of breathing and relaxation exercise, education, imaginal and in vivo exposure and cognitive restructuring was equivalent to that of an eight-session patient treatment. Similarly, Ghosh & Marks (1987) limited the therapy of its self-directed exposure program for agoraphobia to at least three and a maximum of 10 sessions. Results found that this psychiatrist-induced therapy led to major progress in agoraphobic mitigation at six-month follow-up. Due to the fact that their other therapeutic procedures, like a self-help book or electronic manuals, is almost as effective suggests that an awareness program without real contact with the therapist is an acceptable form of treatment. New research, however, challenges the efficacy of mere self-help therapy in the lack of any therapist contact. Notably, neither of these research contrasted abbreviated to unabbreviated CBT and had no effect on comorbid conditions.

Some research explored using telephone contacts to lessen the amount of therapy sessions. Cot'e uv in 1994 delivered 17 individual CBT sessions (such as breathing retraining, education, relaxation, cognitive therapy, interoceptive and sensory exposure) to panic disorder patients or the same treatment over seven sessions and eight short-lived telephone contacts. Findings showed that both treatments were impactful at six-month follow-up, with substantial and comparable improvements. For homebound agoraphobic patients or those removed from treatment facilities, guided exposure therapy involving only telephone contact can also be successful when offered over 8 or 10 telephone sessions. However, this last study recorded high dropout rate for the telephone-guided exposure group.

Direct contrasts between abbreviated and unabbreviated CBT comprise a research by Botella & Garc'ıa-Palacios (1999), who compared a traditional 10-session CBT for panic disorder with an abbreviated 5-session treatment in a group sample with an overall low educational level. Results indicated that treatments were successful and broadly similar, with both groups sustaining improvements over 12-month follow-up. These research results are comparable to those of Newman et al. (1997), who contrasted standard 12-session individual CBT to a 4-session, computer-assisted CBT. Both treatment groups showed significant post-treatment improvement at six-month follow-up. Clinical significance analyses suggested superiority of 12-session condition, but only after treatment. Finally, Clark et al. weighed up a brief five-session cognitive therapy for panic disorder to a standard 12–15-session version of the same treatment. Both were highly successful and preferable to a state of waiting-list monitoring, and there were no major discrepancies between the two treatments. It is interesting that, compared to longer CBT studies, the brief treatment versions listed in the previous three experiments all contained self-help content as an alternative to treatment. Botella & Garc'ıa-Palacios (1999) provided their brief participants with a self-help manual and audiotape, while Clark et al. (1999) also offered written self-study resources and exercises to patients in brief cognitive therapy. Likewise, Newman et al. (1997) provided a computer-assisted therapy feature for all four-session therapy participants. Therefore, it is unknown if the findings would have varied had unabbreviated CBT contained the same self-help content.

A final solution shortens the duration of treatment by delivering intensive treatment in a short period. Evans et al. (1991) delivered a two-day 18-hour intense group CBT. Major symptom improvements were observed for this population relative to a waiting-list control group, and the clinically meaningful progress observed for 85 percent of these patients was sustained at one-year follow-up. But these findings should be viewed carefully as this was not a randomized experiment. In another open study, Spiegel & Barlow (2000) examine an eight-day comprehensive panic disorder recovery plan for mild to serious agoraphobia combining therapist-directed and self-directed communication. The preliminary results are good.

Some studies recorded an individual difference variable of significance to result from brief CBT. Craske et al. discovered that four weekly sessions of abbreviated CBT is preferable to four non-directive therapy sessions for patients seeking pharmacological help. The results were however, not as impactful as usually found with 10-15 CBT sessions, and the less debilitating patients were most improved with this particular abbreviated CBT. Febbraro et al. (1999) discovered that the prevalence of panic disorder diagnoses did not predict outcomes in their studies of people who experience panic attacks with or without panic disorder. The study depicted above by Clark et al. found that treatment at the end of the first session was successful and that the outcome foreseen was predicted by a measure of belief on body feelings after a year follow-up. Evans et al. confirmed that none of its eleven variables for pretreatment anticipated what would happen.

Specific Phobia

A great deal of work has been done to establish brief and effective CBT for various phobias. Treatment usually includes awareness about the essence of the fear; cognitive restructuring of thoughts and misunderstanding of the entity or circumstance being feared, and in vivo exposure and systematic imaginal to the feared entity or situation. Such techniques are used in all forms of phobia, but applied tension is applied in the treatment of injection phobias, blood and wounds. In 1996, Ost investigated the basic outcomes for the treatment of phobia and found levels of clinical progress in just one to eight sessions ranging between 77 and 90%. Treatment studies have included dental phobia, phobias of blood, injury, and injection; claustrophobia; acrophobia; animal phobia; and flying phobia. Ost also studied the long-term outcomes of these studies and found that these gains are typically sustained for up to 10 years following effective therapy.

There are many findings that support the use of single-session therapies for common phobias. For instance, Ost et al. noticed that in spider-phobic patients, one session of therapist-driven exposure lasting a maximum of three hours significantly decreased fear and avoidance. This therapy was superior to a self-managed, two-week exposure program. These researchers later showed that this single-session, therapist-driven treatment is often preferable to manual self-help treatment programs requiring unsupervised patient-driven exposure activities either at home or in the hospital. Single-session therapist-driven exposure therapy is also successful when given in a group setting, particularly if given in smaller groups (i.e., about three to four persons).

Compared with longer-length therapies, single-session CBT is supported for other phobias. Hellstrom et al. (1996) weighed up a single two-hour session to five applied tension treatment sessions that instructed patients to avoid fainting muscle tension response after exposure to injury stimuli and feared blood. A third group of treatments each received a single two-hour tension session without the exposure. All the three groups managed to improve considerably after treatment and follow-up for one year. Though the five sessions applied tension treatment was found to be superior to that of the one-session applied tension treatment at post-treatment, there were no difference in follow-up. They also noticed that individuals categorized as "fainters" changed as much as (and even more so on two measures) those categorized as "non-fainters." This group of researchers also reached the conclusion that the treatment of preference for injection phobia is one single session of therapist-directed exposure (Ost et al., 1992). One therapy session, which did not surpass three hours in duration, was incredibly successful in both post-treatment and follow-up after one year. Additionally, this one-session therapy was just as efficient and effective as the same treatment offered over five sessions. Recent research also shows that one CBT session for claustrophobia is approximately equal to five same-treatment sessions (Ost et al., 2001). Likewise, one three-hour exposure and cognitive rehabilitation session was just as functional as five sessions of the same procedure for flying phobia at post-treatment and one-year follow-up. However, this study recorded some loss in the treatment gains at follow-up for both groups. Clearly, this research body indicates circumscribed phobias are well adapted for brief CBT; and it seems to be as successful in the short term as long term.

Other Anxiety Disorders

Abbreviated treatments for specific phobia and panic disorder (either with or without agoraphobia) have the most empirical support of all anxiety disorders. Some research endorse brief CBT for other forms of anxiety disorders. A growing number of controlled research results support the overall effectiveness of cognitive-behavioral therapies for general anxiety disorder (GAD). Standard CBT treatments typically involve relaxation training, anxiety monitoring, imagery exposure, and cognitive therapy and generally take place over about 12 sessions. That being said, only eight CBT sessions in one study were contrasted with non-directive therapy and a waiting list control situation (Blowers et al., 1987). Results indicates that while CBT has resulted in substantial clinical improvements consistently greater than the waiting-list condition during post-treatment and six months of follow-up, there have been few variations between CBT and non-directive counseling groups. Another research found that a large-group six-session treatment was successful in controlling GAD as opposed to waiting list control, but changes were identical to a "placebo" variant of the treatment. Further research demonstrated that CBT for GAD can be successful in just 4–7 sessions that tend to be approximately equivalent to active treatment and better than medication placebo. A newly evolved CBT method for GAD was successfully performed in six group sessions with the additional use of a palmtop computer system. The study consisted, however, of an unregulated case design with a single group of three persons involved. A direct contrast between abbreviated and unabbreviated CBT for GAD is lacking in the studies till date.

Social phobia may be successfully treated over about 12 sessions of individual or group CBT, and these therapies usually include cognitive restructuring, psychoeducation, and exposure to social situations that cause anxiety (Heimberg & Juster, 1995). Although good structured psychotherapy outcomes research have been developed to support this approach, little knowledge about the effectiveness of abbreviated therapies is available. In an unregulated analysis, Rapee in 1993 presented an abbreviated version of the cognitive-behavioral group treatment put together by Heimberg et al. The therapy consisted of six sessions lasting 90 minutes. The findings showed a substantial increase on most outcome variables at post-treatment and at three- to six-month follow-up. Just 30 of the initial 52 participants had data available, and only one-third of the other participants met strict clinical "responder" requirements at post and follow-up evaluations. Although this improvement rate falls within the expected 20–95% range (Feske & Chambless, 1995), Heimberg and his colleagues reported improvements of about 75% after treatment and 81% at six-month follow-up after unabbreviated CBGT.

The effectiveness of a brief intervention to avoid the onset of post-traumatic stress disorder (PTSD) among women in recent attacks was investigated by Foa et al. (1995). This study group tailored their successful CBT therapy for PTSD to a brief preventive plan consisting of four two-hour person sessions. The findings showed substantial changes in a number of post-treatment and 5.5 months after the attack. Improvements were also greater in some variables than for a similar repeated evaluation control group. Ultimately, only 10% of the CBT participants subsequently met PTSD diagnosis criteria, while 70% of the control group balanced met PTSD criteria. These results should be carefully interpreted because participants have not been distributed randomly. No trials of brief CBT therapy for obsessive-compulsive disorder (OCD) have been found. Standard CBT for OCD is very intense and is usually composed of 15 two-hour sessions taking place every day over a span of three weeks. Such intensive treatment may be essential if an individual is to become adequately exposed to fearful situations without a compulsive response that reinforces fear.

Eating Disorders

Although CBT is popularly used for anorexia nervosa, few randomized controlled research have been written, and treatment usually extends a period of one to two years. In comparison, a number of well-controlled clinical trials support CBT for bulimia nervosa (Wilson et al., 1997), and this procedure has also been modified successfully to combat binge eating disorder too. Abbreviated forms of CBT have been created for binge eating disorder and for bulimia nervosa.

Standard CBT for bulimia nervosa is also entirely focused on the Fairburn et al. (1993) handbook. This treatment plan involves problem-solving and self-control techniques, education, changes in eating behavior, self-monitoring, and cognitive rehabilitation, and is usually delivered over 19 sessions. In a limited, unregulated trial, the procedure was reduced to a total of eight 20-minute sessions in a primary care facility, and 55 percent of patients showed substantial progress. These findings are comparable with a randomized controlled study which discovered eight CBT sessions to be incredibly effective across six-month follow-up and preferable to a self-monitoring procedure with placebo attention.

A few research clearly show that certain bulimic patients may also benefit from brief treatments that prioritize the educational aspect. Olmstead et al. (1991), for example, evaluated by comparing a 19-sessions individual of standard CBT to five-session instructional group treatment for bulimia nervosa. The results showed equal efficacy in the mitigation of symptoms for the least severe 25–45 percent of the sample, while standard CBT was linked with greater improved performance for the more acute participants. This replicates the research findings with panic disorder and agoraphobia. This five-session psychoeducation therapy has also proved to be more successful than waiting-list monitoring and comparable to 12-session CBT group process treatment, although the latter study employed a synchronous cohort design without arbitrary assignment. Nevertheless, in a follow-up review, Davis et al. (1999) contrasted a six-session educational therapy to this same procedure, combined with 16 extra CBT sessions, and discovered some benefit from the longer procedure. While this research contrasted a brief CBT treatment to a longer treatment, there were elements other than those referenced in the brief psychoeducational treatment in the extra sessions in the standard CBT condition.

A second line of study has discovered that the number of binge eating disorder and bulimia nervosa treatment sessions can be decreased with the assistance of self-help resources. In 1994, Treasure et al. weighed up eight CBT sessions after they provided a self-help guide to standard CBT sessions for bulimia nervosa. Post-treatment and 18-month follow-up findings did not show any variations between the two treatment groups, and both were better when compared to a control group on the waiting list. Likewise, unregulated research suggests that when given over as few as four sessions, this guided self-help approach may be efficient. Carter & Fairburn (1998) contrasted non-specialist facilitator-guided self-help and pure self-help treatment to a state of waiting-list control in a broad randomized controlled trial. Both self-help groups received a book focused on CBT treatment for binge eating disorder, and the directed self-help participants met with a mediator for six to eight brief sessions to debate the materials content. The results indicated that both treatment outcomes resulted in significant improvements relative to the waiting-list group, and treatment effects were sustained at a follow-up duration of six months. However, later research has shown the advantages of therapist-guided self-help therapy for binge eating as opposed to an unguided variant of this procedure.

A similar disorder, obesity, can be successfully treated with CBT in 16–20 sessions and a few reports indicate that a computer therapy system can help minimize this treatment. Agras et al. (1990) randomly selected slightly overweight to moderately overweight women to a one-session plus computer therapy, a five-session plus computer therapy, or standard CBT delivered over 10 group sessions. Results showed that at one-year follow-up, the moderate treatment effects were comparable for the three groups. This research group later showed that two different computer treatments, coupled with four group sessions, resulted in huge weight reduction, although one computer group was significantly better than the other. These computer-assisted treatment services tend to be most successful when individuals have been told to use them seven days a week and there is little change in the outcomes by incorporating a brief support group component.

Couples Therapy

A few studies explored the efficacy of reducing traditional 10–20-session CBT in treating couple dysfunction. Halford & Osgarby performed a quasi-experimental analysis contrasting a brief three-session CBT with standard CBT of 12–15 sessions. Both treatments yielded important post-treatment and similar results. Davidson & Horvath supported 40 couples with either three brief CBT sessions that stressed delayed treatment or cognitive reframing. Treatment resulted in substantial progress on some outcome indicators compared with delayed treatment, and the treatment results were sustained at six-month follow-up. Ultimately, in a group of non-treatment-seeking college student couples, a three-session assessment-feedback program led to minor positive improvements and was preferable to a written assessment only treatment.

Alcohol Use

A significant number of treatments have been created for alcoholism, and CBT is considered to be one of the most impactful treatments. CBT treatments for alcohol consumption and dependence disorders typically single out drinking behavior by strengthening cognitive and behavioral coping skills. Patients are trained to cope with both internal events, including alcohol appetite and external events, including social drinking pressure and environmental indicators that trigger the compulsion to drink.

Standard CBT is provided for drinking problem for approximately 12 sessions. Several brief interventions were developed and examined, but these brief interventions usually involve self-help materials or guidance from primary health care professionals. Bien et al. (1993) examined brief treatments for alcohol problems and found that medical advice interventions are nearly equivalent to standard CBT and other comprehensive treatments. They also revealed that brief inspirational induction treatments seem effective in promoting further therapy for alcoholic patients. CBT has often been a comprehensive treatment that compares other types of brief treatment (i.e., lowest possible physician consultation). However, one research contrasted a self-help bibliotherapy procedure to three brief therapeutic interventions. The first therapeutic treatment group obtained a guided self-help variant of the bibliotherapy intervention in six sessions. The second treatment group obtained six coping skills training sessions in which techniques were taught and practiced to deal with high-risk situations. The last therapist-directed treatment group obtained a combination of both treatments over eight sessions. The results showed a significant decrease in the weekly consumption of alcohol in all four groups and these improvements were maintained at a one-year follow-up. There were no significant differences between the groups.

Sobell & Sobell (1993) also abbreviated CBT for drinking problem. Their guided self-management therapy program is designed to inspire change in behavior as well as provide initiatives and strategies to achieve behavioral objectives. Treatment procedures typically involve setting goals for drinking behavior therapy, self-monitoring alcohol education, identifying triggers and drinking consequences, and developing behavioral strategies for achieving set goals. Although the treatment duration is flexible enough to meet the individual requirements, this guided self-management therapy can be successfully implemented in two sessions. A randomly selected treatment outcomes investigation compared two 90-minute behavioral component sessions with just two 90-minute behavioral plus cognitive recurrence prevention sessions. The results showed that the drinking behavior reported in both groups was significantly reduced. These results have been maintained at a follow-up period of six and 12 months. There were no differences between the two treatments.

Marlatt and colleagues developed a one-session intervention in high-risk college students to avoid drinking problems. In the winter term of her first year, Marlatt et al. (1998) designated a random assignment for college freshmen to either obtain an individual interview session or no treatment at all. Participants deemed to have the highest likelihood (based on reported secondary school drinking behavior) of alcohol-related problem development were chosen. The treatment consists of a revision of the self-monitoring of drinking habit by the participants, individualized feedback on reported drinking patterns, associated risk and alcohol beliefs; conversations of information and misunderstandings on alcohol impacts; and risk reduction suggestions. The purpose of this intervention was to increase motivation and to avoid judgmental or confrontational comments. The results showed decreases in drinking rates and detrimental effects for both groups over a follow-up period of two years, but the treatment benefits for the intervention group were substantially higher.

Pain Management

This section focuses on brief treatments study for low back pain and headache, although there are effective CBT-oriented treatments for a wide variety of chronic pain conditions. CBT programs are universally used, effective methods of headache pain management. Treatment usually involves relaxation training (for example, progressive relaxation of muscle, meditation and autogenic training) and/or biofeedback, education and cognitive coping. Over the past decade , researchers have established brief treatments called minimum therapist contact, with only three to five sessions of CBT administered. In 1996, Rowan & Andrasik methodically evaluated the controlled results study available to investigate the effectiveness of the minimum CTB therapist contact for headache pain. Two studies revealed that three sessions are can be compared to 10 relaxation training sessions for adult stress-type headache. In three relaxation sessions, equivalent effectiveness was also demonstrated in relation to five relaxation sessions plus cognitive therapy, and to 11 relaxation and cognitive treatment sessions. However, one study showed some benefits of a three-session treatment, which included both cognitive and relaxation treatment, for just three relaxation sessions. Minimal therapist CBT contact for headache tension has also proved superior to a waiting list control and comparable with a medication of amitriptyline. Rowan & Andrasik (1996) deduced that these brief tension headache therapies, consisting mainly of progressive muscle relief workouts, are as efficacious as long clinical relaxation workouts. 37-50 percent of participants have strictly improved clinically after the treatment and up to two years of follow-up.

Also described by Rowan & Andrasik (1996) are several other studies that support vascular headaches of minimal CBT therapist contact. Williamson et al. found, for example, that four group relaxation training sessions corresponded to eight group workshops, with both of these treatments improving significantly when contrasted to placebo. Likewise, three sessions of individual relaxation treatment were discovered to be remarkably similar to 16 sessions for both pure migraine and migraine coupled with tension-type headache participants. Individual relaxation in three sessions with the addition of thermal biofeedback proves to be equal to 16 sessions of the treatment, three abortive medicine and compliance intervention sessions, and five different sessions of the same treatment with the addition of cognitive therapy. This therapy was also better in comparison to headache-monitoring condition. Richardson & McGrath eventually discovered that only two CBT sessions brought about the same effects as an eight CBT session, and both were better in comparison to the waiting-list control. Rowan & Andrasik concluded from these studies that brief relaxation treatments, with or without thermal biofeedback, is as successful as longer therapy treatments, which results in a clinically important improvement in 40 to 79 percent of patients.

A couple of studies encourage the usage of minimal therapist contact in children and teenagers with headaches. Three relaxation training sessions were discovered to be superior to two nine-session of a headache monitoring sessions with adolescent tension headache and an attention placebo condition. Three and four sessions of thermal biofeedback therapy also seem equivalent to 10 sessions in children between eight and sixteen years of age for the treatment of vascular headaches. After that, one CBT session with extra therapist telephone contact was nearly equivalent to eight CBT sessions and vastly better to the waiting list control in a group of eleven to eighteen-year-old migraine patients.

Judith Turner and colleagues have produced efficacious brief CBT procedures for chronic low back pain treatment in older people. Early research has shown that five 90-minute CBT group sessions are comparable to five relaxation sessions for the majority of post-treatment measurements, with certain advantages for CBT groups of up to two years after therapy. When an eight-session behavioral group treatment targeted at changing problematic "pain behaviors" was contrasted with an eight-session CBT group treatment, both treatments improved significantly and equivalently with one-year follow up in comparison to the waiting list control. In conjunction with an exercise component, this eight-session behavioral treatment also showed a greater advancement than eight sessions in both components after treatment. All of the three treatments were found to be more effective better the waiting list control, and all three were comparable at six months and one year follow up. Likewise, six-session CBT combining the elements, six-session cognitive therapy, and six-session relaxation training resulted in significant and similar pain intensity cuts in comparison to the waiting list control. These improvements were maintained both for six months and one year in all of the three treatment groups.

Many controlled research studies endorse the use of abbreviated CBT in a number of specific phobias as well as in panic disorder treatment (either with or without agoraphobia). Preliminary studies suggest that brief CBT therapies may also be useful for treating GAD, social phobia, and for preventing PTSD after assault. Early efforts were made to reduce the length of depression therapy for both adults and children. Decreased session treatment is efficacious for both binge eating disorders and bulimia nervosa in the zone of eating disorders with several studies that support the use of brief computer-aided therapies to help reduce weight gain and obesity. Some research has also indicated that couples can abbreviate CBT therapy and yield positive results. Whilst a large amount of research endorses the effectiveness of CBT for alcohol disorders, short treatments do not typically include components of CBT therapy. However, one CBT treatment has been shortened to two sessions, and the results are promising. A similar one-session procedure seems useful in the elimination of alcohol-related predicament in college students. Ultimately, a wide range of research endorses the use of lowest possible therapist contact treatment for headache, and new meta-analysis has shown that these treatments are continually similar to longer, clinically based treatments. Lowest possible therapist contact treatment for headache also seems efficacious for children and adolescents. A series of research investigations also endorses the usage of abbreviated CBT for chronic low-back pain.

These research results generally support the abbreviation practice of the CBT standard. However, certain conditions were much more studied than others. Circumstances with specific, limited, maladaptive characteristics and symptoms may be more appropriate for this methodology. Specific phobias are, in fact the only disorders that have championed the use of brief CBT against unabbreviated CBT in unfounded comparisons. When the maladaptive behavior source can be easily spotted and treated, brief methods are suitable. If the patient is suffering from a wide range of complicated maladaptive thoughts and conduct, a longer treatment may be required. This could explain why a few clinical sessions can accurately treat clinical issues like specific phobia, panic disorders or pain, whereas other disorders including GAD and depression warrant even more study. We need more studies that measures up brief and standard CBT, especially in various disorders, to better help determine those that gain the most from an abbreviated approach, to identify therapeutic change mechanisms and to evaluate the influence that therapeutic variables have on results.

Chapter 2 - Cognitive And Behavioral Techniques

This segment explains in-depth the key cognitive and behavioral strategies used in therapy. The strategies can be adapted to both core and elective topics, but specific strategies can be especially useful for some of the topics that will be listed. Some strategies can work better for some patients than others, thereby increasing treatment versatility and adaptability to take specific patients into account. The strategies were split up into cognitive and behavioral classes based on the focal point of the treatment, but this does not reflect the order of use. Both cognitive and behavioral strategies are used from the beginning.

The order in which the strategies in each section of the book are described should be used for treatment guideline, with some being used throughout the treatment process, while others may be best suited for earlier and/or later treatment stages or superficial or more detailed analysis. For instance, early-stage or superficial cognitive strategies include managing uneasiness and enhancing motivation and everyday thought record; and behavioral strategies include relaxation training and physical activity. Later or deeper cognitive strategies include imagery and downward arrow exercise, as well as behavioral strategies like behavioral experiments. While each procedure is defined independently, there may be an overlap, and several techniques can be used to solve a problem. Circumstances may be used as a merit in combination of techniques.

It is crucial to know that cognitive behavior therapy is not just a set of strategies that can be implemented in a 'cookbook' approach from a food list. Cognitive-behavioral therapy is a tactical approach predicated on the knowledge of cognitive and behavioral science that enables a therapist to comprehend the clinical problems of the patient and to arrange the information in a rational and medically useful way. The formulation is an interpretation of clinical issues by the therapist, which makes it easier to choose an intervention plan. The development of a case formula usually involves the development of a number of clinical hypotheses which are tested by different intervention or treatment methods. In conjunction with the client, it is also necessary to establish the formulation so that the client understands the cognitive-behavioral framework.

Out-Of-Session Assignments

The treatment takes place during therapy sessions as well as during the daily life of the client, at first through home-based workouts but eventually through change in the way of life, which involves changes in the behavior and thinking patterns of the client. The therapist should be aware of this and prepare for long-lasting change, which may include being mindful of how the individual lives and operates and how this can help or discourage a change in lifestyle. Generalizing the skills acquired in therapy in daily life must be thought about and communicated with the client as a problem-solving activity. Client should define factors that will promote and prevent change and prospective solutions developed and implemented. Out-of-session activities will be designed to help generalize and sustain the improvement that has been achieved during therapy sessions. This practice is still poorly conducted, so it should be clarified at an early stage with clients to be informed of it and to encourage an honest evaluation of any potential problems. Initial exercises should be easy, quick to execute, clearly defined and easily monitored so that both the client and therapist will know when they're successfully completed and what their effect is. From the outset, the client's behavior needs to be influenced, which means any approach to completing the exercise needs to be validated by gratitude and direct feedback. Out-of-session tasks expand the therapy to the daily life of the client and are important for the effectiveness of the therapy, given their slow progress. Therefore, careful consideration and discussion are required as to what task is assigned and when and how it is carried out. It is important to avoid overloading or demoralizing the client, complicated or too ambiguous exercises should be avoided, particularly during early treatment stage when it may be impossible to be implemented.

List of Techniques

Cognitive techniques:

- Socratic method

- Daily thought record

- Advantages/disadvantages analysis

- Flashcards

- Downward arrow exercise

- Distraction

- Addressing ambivalence and increasing motivation

- Imagery

Behavioral techniques:

- Contingency management.

- Physical exercise and relaxation training

  - Behavioral rehearsal (role-play and reverse role-play)

- o Behavioral experiments
- Activity-monitoring schedule

Cognitive techniques

Addressing Ambivalence And Increasing Motivation

An investigation of the ambivalence and motivation of the client should be included in the evaluation and communicated as required during the treatment. interventions focused partly on the change model of Prochaska and DiClemente were recounted as 'motivational interviews' by Miller and Rollnick (1992). This approach is primarily intended to deal with the client's understanding of substance use rather than to force the therapist's objective interpretation of reality on the client. Clients are hardly ever in a position where they do not perceive some dimensions of their substance use as inappropriate or in need of improvement, they are given motivation to help them think about the significance of the drug in their life. However, the denial can manifest as defensive mechanism when the therapist challenges the person's opinion. In motivational interviews, the goal is to help consumers discover the negative and positive elements of their use of drugs and develop discrepancies, in order to set out the objectives to change their use of the substance. This latter approach is intended to help customers understand the difference between themselves and their actions (for instance, an alcoholic who sees himself as a 'social drinker' but was investigated for assaulting his partner when he was alcohol-intoxicated).

The procedure vary depending on the stage of change of the client. There are five phases of transition according to Prochaska and DiClemente (1992):

<u>Pre-contemplative stage</u>: The individual is not aware of the issues of alcohol or drug use, so they are often shocked instead of defensive that the issue is being brought up. The objective now is to raise awareness of potential issues.

<u>Contemplative stage</u>: The individual develops a problem consciousness but is ambivalent to change. The goal is to assist the client make a decision that balance adjustment is necessary.

<u>Determination stage</u>: In particular, the therapist supports the patient in accessing the most suitable type of aid in rehabilitation by offering opportunities for improvement (e.g., treatment provider choice) and planning realistic changes (e.g., scheduling time off work, childcare).

<u>Action stage</u>: A variety of intervention options can be used, but typically the customer at this point is involved in the change process, and little guidance is needed in terms of motivation, except to improve the good judgment and commitment of the client.

<u>Maintenance stage</u>: The primary objective of therapy is on detecting strategies of consolidating gains and prevention of relapse. This also includes recognizing changes to long-term lifestyles for keeping changes going. If relapse happens, the procedure is intended to allow the individual to reengage.

Socratic Method

The Socratic approach is a guided process where the therapist encourages self-discovery and awareness. It was based on the method of the ancient Greek philosopher, Socrates, who tried to uncover the truth by attempting to answer questions with questions until the assenter is able to provide an answer to their own inquiry. It creates an unjustified environment and therefore promotes communication between the client and the therapist. Active questioning and selective reflection shape your thinking. It enables an individual to become conscious of their own beliefs and conduct. By asking these questions, an individual may develop a better understanding of their thoughts processes and how feelings and actions are influenced. The client thus become conscious of unbefitting beliefs and is encouraged to challenge them and improve their conduct. Clarification, suggestions, and education centered on the subject of the discussion will complement the guided questioning. Questions should be formulated in a way that thought and perception are enhanced instead of expecting an accurate answer. It can be questions that identify the relationship between thoughts and emotions, particularly if negative automatic thoughts are concerned. For instance, the client may think that he "will never again be normal," and he is asked to explain how he starts to feel when he has this viewpoint. The therapist will then discuss the relevance and the utility of this thought with the client, but this is not accomplished by explicitly challenging the thought. The philosophies of collaborative empiricism are valued by asking questions that confirm or oppose the belief, by asking questions about potential alternative interpretations, by challenging the range of consequences of thought and its impact on the individual and how they can be believed or modified.

Daily Thought Record

The daily thought record is aimed at encouraging clients to thoroughly and critically evaluate their own drug-related beliefs or other ideas. It also enables the therapist to understand the thought processes of the client. This is normally achieved by a table divided into six columns, which include emotions, response, outcome, rational response, situation, and automatic thoughts/beliefs. The goal is for the client to recognize and document circumstances (external events, such as actions, places, incidents, and times) or emotional factors that precipitate drug consumption. This helps the client and therapist to look at the process that contributes to the use of drugs and, thus, to change thought and behavior. The purpose of this exercise is primarily to assist the client and therapist in recognizing internal (feelings) and external (circumstances) substance triggers, related attitudes and thought and behavior patterns connected with them. Secondly, the exercise offers knowledge essential for educating clients on the cognitive model and helps them to understand that drug abuse is a decision-making mechanism where they can make their own choice. Thirdly, it helps clients to become conscious of their thoughts processes and connect them with behavior and emotions. This method has the added benefit of having some "distance" from the thoughts in order to delay and potentially regulate the emotional reaction. Clients should also be conscious of their emotions and thoughts and how they are connected instead of being "trapped" in their thoughts.

The notebook also offers useful scenarios for training skills using the client's own examples. Individuals are able to track their growth, increase motivation, and self-efficacy through self-learning and self-monitoring.

Distraction

Distraction may allow individuals to focus solely on either internal (automatic thinking, craving, emotional) and external drug-related stimuli. Distraction may be cognitive or behavioral (physical exercise, house chores, and gardening). Cognitive distraction includes teaching individuals to distract themselves away from drugs and to concentrate their thoughts on certain things, such as describing environments. The ability to control and monitor attention is essential. The client will have multiple distraction techniques, which should be client-specific, to be used in various circumstances. Systematic training in the control of attention and attention switching can be accomplished by asking the individual to discuss different aspects or items in their environment and by concentrating on it for a particular period of time. Take objects or images in a house, for example, and then outside noises, like traffic. This helps clients control and monitor their attention processes. Then, by creating an appropriate visual image or a position or circumstance, the consumer may be asked to focus on inner stimuli. These can be fun, calming pictures like a tropical beach, or a positive experience that honors the client, including a meal or a steakhouse. The client will then explain the situation in extensive detail and construct a vivid mental picture. This is done many times until the client can clearly and easily develop the mental image. The client could also imagine other sensory aspects, such as how he felt like he was at sunshine on the beaches, wave movement and the feel of sand etc. Through the demand for positive information about the situation, all senses are actively engaged and strongly linked to the positive impact by producing optimistic emotional answers. Customers are then trained to turn their focus from a number of other stimuli to the objective scenario until they are highly qualified to do so. When they are able to do that, they can use this internal distraction and attention-changing strategy to respond to unwanted thoughts and emotions. Thoughts regarding improved controls should be encouraged to improve these behaviors, develop the self-effectiveness feelings of the client and reduce the assumption of the resilience of drug-related experience and perceptions. Distraction can also be accomplished by behaviors that re-focus attention on these tasks. The patient will easily implement and use these specific behavioral exercises in earlier stages of therapy as an active coping mechanism rather than as strictly cognitive tasks. It is beneficial for the client to participate in specific activities as a form of distraction because they need active focus and in doing so reducing the attention capacity for drug-related thoughts. Client's habits and other interests can also help to change lifestyle choices. It is crucial that clients have a variety of cognitive and behavioral strategies as they can be found in situations where certain activities are not possible, such as repeated situations in which the customers feel bored and then starts to think of drugs which bring about craving. The client must also know that distraction may also be used to contradict negative thinking or perceptions, for example, 'I can't control my actions' or 'I will never change.

Advantages/Disadvantages Analysis

This includes listing the benefits and drawbacks of substance use and overall reassessment of using drugs. The benefits and drawbacks of using and not using drugs are accomplished with a four-cell matrix. The exercise can be included in the session or as a non-session exercise. It is essential that the client shares his own opinion about advantages and disadvantages of substance abuse rather than the therapist or society in general so that cognitive assessment can allow the client to accurately reflect his views. This task is useful in order to enable clients, through their analysis of the issue, to develop alternative views and challenge assumptions. If the analysis works, the client would have a more precise, unbiased and realistic view of substance use than before. Statements created by this strategy can be used as a material for other techniques including downward arrow exercise or flashcards and , as part of any session can aid in setting goals and increasing motivation.

Flashcards

Flashcards actually assist clients to use what they experience in real-life scenarios in therapy. In a stimulus situation, clients have to learn how to face and deal with their unconscious thinking and drug-related convictions, they have to remind themselves of how to overcome these thoughts and/or figure out how to deal. These may be suitable reactions to challenges, coping assertions, or validation of positive outcomes of being drug-free. Flashcards should be lightweight, suitable to transport, and should include the client's own relevant statements. Flashcards can be used in a variety of situations and for multiple functions like memory aids, challenge unacceptable thought patterns and to help achieve and direct goal-oriented conduct and positive action. They are also an external reference point for creating a suitable inner dialogue and for prompting relevant beliefs and cognitions. In an atmosphere in which the cues are most possibly linked to unhealthy beliefs or drug use, effective self-talks may be very valuable in the self-direction of actions. It is important to note that they should be focused and working.

Downward Arrow Exercise

Clients are almost always unfamiliar with their own core beliefs, or they may find it difficult to express the accessible or suitable beliefs and thoughts they experience in terms of their personal meaning (i.e., what does that connote to you). The underlying beliefs are highly likely to reflect existing cognition that the client may become conscious of or learn to become conscious of. By using the Socratic questioning technique, clients are allowed to reach these underlying fundamental beliefs by asking questions about their thoughts. Using this approach, clients may become conscious of or embrace underlying fears or concerns. In the absence of their conscience, these beliefs also drive their behavior. The downward arrow is a useful way to reach core beliefs by asking several alteration to the question, "what does that imply to you?' or 'what would it imply if that was necessarily the case?'. Instances of this include: de-catastrophizing (e.g., "What is the worst thing that can occur here?"); the correcting "all or nothing" thought (e.g. "I'm totally out of hand"). Overgeneralization (e.g., "I can't just do anything right"). This procedure should not be used outside of the session, so it should be rehearsed and exercised during the therapy session under the guidance of the therapist. Information collected from the exercise may be used as a wakeup call for the client outside the therapy session for other strategies or on flashcards. The technique often reveals the irrational or ambiguous nature of the client's beliefs or does not take account of other alternatives or explanations of events. This lack of cognitive versatility can be used as a therapeutic tool to encourage the client to consider various solutions or perceptions at all times.

Imagery

Imagery as a tool involves making the client think of particular problems related to drugs or alcohol can be used retroactively to 'commemorate' a past experience in order to track down the feelings, ideas, and meanings associated with the experience. For instance, a retroactive situation and the reason for why drinking has been revived are defined may also be used to formulate an appropriate coping strategy for a 'project ahead' in a challenging situation. It can as well be used to over-learn coping mechanisms in order to make them easier to implement.

Imagery is a helpful way to help clients visualize daily scenarios and potential consequences during therapy. This is achieved by allowing them to relive the memory like it is happening here and now. Mental images alone are strong flashbacks but can be further strengthened when clients relive their experiences by using all their senses. Asking the client how something tasted, smelt, felt or any related sounds helps to relive all the senses, through visual imagery is perhaps the strongest. In this way, cognitive mechanisms and affective and emotional responses can be categorized into drug or alcohol-related beliefs, unconscious thought, action-oriented attitudes and associated sensations may be used as an alternative or as a daily record of thought. It also may be helpful for people who are not very good at keeping diaries. Additionally, imagery can be an effective tool to challenge thought and values, and to visualize alternate methods for coping. It is as well very useful in the rehearsal of specific coping strategies, the identification of positive results and possible impediments. This may also be used to help the client look at the positive side of a drug-free way of living. For example, consider recreational activities as alternative options to drug use and visualize life without drugs and anticipate positive feelings that such way of life would bring. For clients who have nothing to draw upon from their previous successful drug-free experience, it is crucial to emphasize the positive side of being drug-free. Positive thinking can also be a brilliant way to develop clients' self-esteem by asking them to picture a positive image or series of behaviors and by eliciting positive feedbacks about themselves. It can be further improved by urging the customer to try to replicate the positive impact of the encounter. In the future, cued images can be used to induce positive results and emotions about yourself and to invoke positive behavior.

Imagery can't be conveyed as effectively as possible, but it can only be used when the therapist and client feel relaxed and confident enough to do so. Mental images are also a good indicator of emotions, sometimes more than words or explanations, and they can inadvertently activate strong emotions. This means offering the client an educated strategy explanation and assessing their emotional state prior to commencement.

Behavioral Techniques

Activity-Monitoring Schedule

The monitoring and scheduling of activities could be useful strategies to fully comprehend drug and alcohol behaviors, as well as to improve productive behavior. This gives an overview of the activities of the client, a summary of alcohol or drug use, and shows where activities can be altered to obtain a positive benefit. This takes place through a blank grid, which is separated into 7 days of the week and then divided into 1-hour blocks. For a duration of 1 week, the client records daily activities and the degree to which each activity has a feeling of pleasure or mastery taking part in each activity. This can be recorded in a visual analog scale from 1 to 10 by the client.

The uses of the daily program are:

- Journal of current activities - to gain a basic knowledge of current activities and how they connect to the use of drugs.

- Potential guide for future activities-can be used to plan fewer and/or more pleasant future activities relating to drugs and alcohol.

- Assessing to what extent the client has successfully followed the planned schedule.

Relaxation Training And Physical Exercise

The therapist may encourage them, especially for outside the therapy session.

Relaxation Training

This could be useful because it provides the customer with a safe (drug-free) relaxation approach. It also gives the customer a time lag following the original craving experience during which the hankering can decrease. There are various relaxation techniques, including rapid relaxation, progressive relaxation, differential relaxation, cue-controlled relaxation and release only relaxation. Also extremely helpful are relaxation techniques that can provide a feeling of control or mastery over anxiety or craving feelings and can be utilized to challenge elementary beliefs that embellish the physical feelings or expectation that improvements or changes are not possible. t is crucial to be able to relax and feel comfortable, but clients may equate drugs or alcohol use with feeling relaxed. It is necessary to investigate the significance of relaxation and, if required, address beliefs. For example, helping your client to find and connect other non-drugs-related behaviors with relaxation. Some nervous clients may feel uneasy when trying to relax because it makes them feel like they are about to lose control. In most cases, graded practice and reassurance can overcome this, whilst also identifying and testing the negative and outrageous expectations.

Physical Exercise

The therapist may motivate the client in the course of the treatment to engage in physical exercise. This can help customers reinvent themselves as physically active people. The image should trigger clients to experience cognitive dissonance and may encourage them to adjust the pattern of substance abuse. The client can also cope with forbearance, anxiety and other external stimuli. Physical exercise is also a good distraction and breaks down negative ruminative thinking cycles. Physical exercise should be developed progressively in light of the fitness and health level of the client. Where appropriate, medical guidance should be sought.

Behavioral Rehearsal (Role-Play And Reverse Role-Play)

Behavioral rehearsal is a technique that can be used in therapy to illuminate any relationship problem the client cannot clarify or cope with to the therapist. In that case, the customer can play the role of problematic others and the therapist can play the role of the client. It can as well be used to try-out and practice more efficacious or adaptive communication skills to deal with various situations in which the therapist takes on the part of another person and the client can use more powerful techniques of communication in a secure environment in which errors can be corrected without actual repercussions. The teaching component which the client and the therapist take in assessing a situation and discuss more efficient or adaptive responses are as essential as the role-play exercise. This technique is usually preceded by relevant behavioral experiments as it is exercised under secure environments. Rehearsal through imagery or through actual conduct is very crucial for the acquisition of new skills and coping methods. The discussion may lead to the customer being informed about what to do but with very little practice. This may well lead to failure in real-life circumstances, just as the instruction on how to ride a bicycle is a poor replacement for the actual practice of biking. Practice is extremely beneficial as it helps identify previously unanticipated factors, like negative cognitions, and to achieve new behavior through physical practice. Overlearning is a great strategy in relation to the latter. This is when practice goes far beyond new behavior during the session. This is on the grounds that the acquired skills will fade and the actual situation will always vary greatly or create unexpected challenges in comparison with the training situation.

Behavioral Experiments

Behavioral experiments are used to assess the ability of client to challenge their drug or alcoholic beliefs, their fundamental values and exercise their newly acquired adaptive coping skills. The entire point of this procedure is that it is an experiment used to determine whether a certain belief is correct or not. This is based on the impression that clients maintain belief or expectations that are not entirely inaccurate, but because of misconceptions about thought (like the selection of certain information and events instead of others), or the use of safety behavior (so that the belief can be strengthened or not shown to be erroneous), these unbefitting beliefs are reinforced and not contested. A behavioral experiment involves trying to manipulate a situation in order to challenge and disapprove of a wrong or distasteful belief. An unsuitable belief is identified and the client is motivated to indicate what will happen in a given situation if it is true and to prognosticate what would happen if it is wrong. The experiment is a conduct test of the client's inappropriate conviction of two conflicting hypotheses. The client is then motivated to perform the experiment, see what goes on and take lessons from it. The client most often needs significant assistance at first through the therapist's instructions, but the practice should be reiterated until the client can generate independent ways to assess beliefs.

Behavioral experiments are incredibly beneficial if an effective response and associated behavioral change occurs. Like if anxiety is connected with avoidance. This almost always shows a type of catastrophic thinking or expectation which can be tested by asking customers to change their behavior.

Behavioral experiments can be performed in two different ways:

- In real circumstances: For instance, a customer might be convinced that "he cannot decline drugs" and be asked to reveal himself to a drug stimulus like going past his or her house. They can be helped by applying the techniques they have tested to cope with these scenarios. Thus, clients are able to test themselves in challenging their fundamental or drug-related beliefs in a vulnerable situation and thus enhance their self-efficacy. Behavioral experiments can be used to evaluate the true reality and legitimacy of any maladaptive ideas. This way, you can identify the thought and isolate it from all emotions, for example, by just jotting down the thought. The client can make several predictions following this idea, inspired by the therapist. These predictions are generally intense or catastrophic, like 'I'm always going to fail' or 'I'm going to go mad if I do that.' The therapist focuses on building on these intense predictions and help the client experiment in order to invalidate the prediction and to prove it to be wrong.

- The therapist inquires the client to envision that she is in a desired circumstance and to act as if a certain number of circumstances were true. This activity can help to change behavior and lifestyle. The "as if" technique should be used for carefully orchestrated testing or when it is unpractical to be exposed to real situations.

Experiments can be used for any treatment to test unsuitable beliefs, but as treatment advances they should become more powerful and efficient. Behavioral assessments requiring exposure to actual drugs or alcohol conditions should be performed later on in the experiment when the person is comfortable enough and all approaches have been rehearsed and integrated. Exposure should be rated, the client should assess vulnerability circumstances and start with the least challenging. Each stage should be solidified before attempting to move on to the next stage. If the procedure is unsuccessful, and the client degenerates, the therapist has to motivate the client to continue pursuing the therapy by reviewing the incident and to learn from the experience by reassessing what went wrong.

A number of behavioral experiments are often necessary to bring about sustainable cognitive change. Clients often indulge in 'protection of hypotheses,' thus overlooking evidence that is not true to their convictions and selecting supporting evidence. When this cognitive distortion happens, selective attention can be indicated and used as a useful example. Thus, numerous behavioral experiments are normally required and their results are continually referenced, so that the insurmountable evidence supports a reasonable point of view and challenges the beliefs of the client. Clients can also participate in the "Yes, but.....' argument against proof and conclusions arising from the behavioral experiment. This can perhaps be pointed out and the consumer taught self-instruction to concentrate on the essential part of the experiment.

Contingency Management

Contingency management, also referred to as incentive, positive reinforcement approaches is a technique largely dependent on operational conditioning principles, which allows clients to receive rewards for particular behaviors, e.g., attendance to group, drug-free urine testing. Contingency management aims to make behavioral changes easier and to provide clear and achievable behavioral objectives for the client. This can be accomplished by upholding operational learning concepts such as timing incentives and aiming incentives at reducing one form of action, for example, by minimizing the usage of one drug instead of many.

Although there is no particular model, there are however four general principles for the implementation of the contingency management model in a therapeutic environment: (i) frequent monitoring is important to ensure that the client adheres to the therapy program; (ii) the therapist and the client agree that no incentive will be granted if the client does not obey the treatment plan; (iii) the therapist and client work with each other to establish appropriate alternative programs for the client; (iv) the offering and withdrawing of incentives must be concordant.

The therapist and the client will discuss the appropriate forms of compensation for the patient, this can be researched in some depth to establish a workable program. If other workers or family members are fully engaged, it must be made sure that they all understand how the system works. A reward should continually and immediately be given on successfully completing of a reward task, such as attendance to a group session and drug-free urine. Based on the nature of the incentive, certain immediate rewards will need to be a certificate acknowledging that the client has earned a reward that will be awarded later. Rewards will be raised in accordance with the number of successful consecutive tasks performed during the treatment. If the client fails to complete a reward task, the schedule of reinforcement must be reset. With continuous success, the schedule can be progressively removed during the treatment process. The client will ideally begin to realize the benefits of treatment as the contingency management plan is phased out, and these will themselves be incentives.

Effort showcased in coordinating issues which would emerge on reaching the end of in-patient treatment (training, housing, personal relationships, work, education). This will vary between clients and should be decided at the first meeting.

Some common problems that have been reported include:

- The incentive given for just one action cannot treat the client as a whole and does not impact behaviors other than the particular behavioral purpose of the incentive.

- Designing an incentive system that would work for the client is the rewards that must be enticing enough to be earned by the client but at the same time not too expensive for the service. Cost was one of the limitations of this strategy.

- A limited or incomplete understanding and execution of the technique would not be successful in this context.

- While it may be helpful to support clients with difficulties in retaining confidence and accepting responsibility in the early phases of their therapy, it is wrong to make it a constant "crutch" or "prop," on which the client is too heavily reliant. The ultimate objective should be that clients build a sense of identity and responsibility for their lives so that decisions can be made about using without depending on schedules that provide incentives that are not part of their daily life.

Chapter 3 - Managing Anxiety

The Internet has approximately 46.5 million responses to the definition of anxiety! In order not to go through all of them in this section, we condense it to the important components:

- What it is?

- Where it comes from?

- What shape it takes?

- What you can DO about it?

Anxiety is often defined as a sense of worry, trepidation or fear. But it's a lot more than just a sensation. It involves feelings or emotions, perceptions and physical sensations.

Occasional anxiety in our everyday life is completely natural. If you have never felt nervous, ever, it should be a matter of concern! Life confronts us with problems that we don't always believe we can handle, so a feeling of anxiety is normal. The challenges can be traumatic situations, like actual danger, occurrence in the actual life and/or things that our minds made up, such as what happens in a catastrophe.

Feelings Or Emotions

We generally feel frightened when we encounter extreme anxiety. Although it is often very easy to recognize what we are afraid of, we get an intense sense of fear at other times. But it depends primarily on your temperament and the sense whether you love or hate this feeling.

Believe it or not some people are looking for powerful sensations and often the stronger the better for these people! Experiencing high levels of anxiety can be enjoyable, even if that might sound strange. Think of horror movies, fun parks and holidays in 'extreme sports.' Some people like the rush of adrenaline that these activities bring. The point is that the enjoyment is typically linked to the time, location and activity you have selected. They will probably be less excited about something that happened uninvited, unexpected, uncontrolled and genuinely dangerous for them!

Thoughts

We generally all try to understand our surroundings and what happens to us. It can be really scary not to know what is going on and to envisage that anything that whatever will happen next may be even worse. Anyone with feelings of fear and anxiety will typically try to find out why and what it implies. How we understand our environment tells us whether it's safe or risky. Shakespeare summarized this intelligently, when he wrote in Hamlet, "there is nothing either good or nothing bad, but thinking does it."

Thus, the connection between emotions and thoughts is already evident - you will probably be seriously frightened if you think anything is really life-threatening. People watching a scary movie are less inclined to enjoy it as they start searching for monsters and aliens as they leave the theater, while people who understand that it is just a "make-believe" are safe to appreciate the scariness inside the movie theatre, realizing there is no such danger in real life.

Bodily Sensations

It can be fascinating to learn how various emotions can be caused by anxiety and also how many parts of the body are significantly impacted. You can only get a few or most of them. The most prominent sensations are:

- You may shudder or have shaking legs and arms.

- You may have icy cold hands and feet.

- You may have a dry throat.

- You may start sweating effusively.

- You may feel you are 'not here,' or you might feel you are out of your body somehow, looking down on everything, distanced from the environment.

- You may feel as if everything is very absolutely incredible.

- You can feel dizzy, tired or lightheaded.

- You can feel like you have a lump in your throat or that you can't just swallow.

- You may feel nauseous, may even vomiting.

- You may have muscle twitching.

- You can have to go to the bathroom or have a churning stomach.

- You might have a dreadful headache.

- Your heart may beat harder and faster.

- Your chest may feel tight or excruciating.

- You can be nervous, anxious or incapable of relaxing.

- You may have overall pains and aches.

As we said, it is normal to have anxiety when we feel that we are at risk. The 'Triple F' reaction, Fight, Flight or Freeze is the response of your body. This is a truly essential reflex response

– the body does it independently. The 3 Fs are related to our species' survival over the generations. Take the instance of upsetting a hungry wild animals in the bush. Depending on both you and the animal form, you can try to fight it, run away as quickly as you can and stay on hold in the hope that it has a bad eye and will not bother you. Which of the 3 Fs would you count on?

In conditions where you see things as dangerous, the body releases a whole range of chemicals (as well as adrenaline) that causes all of the above physical symptoms. Such physical changes allowed the human race to thrive. The released chemicals cause physical changes, which make it possible for us to function much faster and have a better chance of protecting ourselves and our loved ones in general. This is nice for an objective dangers like a wild animals, but not especially helpful if the perceived danger is more of a psychological one, like being afraid that you will make yourself feel stupid or fear of a physical disaster such as a cardiac arrest or a brain hemorrhaging.

We will discuss various forms of anxiety disorder in a moment. Each links to a variety of thoughts about what is going on. For example, if you suffer from panic attacks you probably fear something awful, like a cardiac arrest or a brain aneurysm, will take place when you experience it, or you are going to get overly emotional and make yourself a total fool. When your condition is an obsessive-compulsive disorder, your fear may be that if you do not do something in the right order, clean or examine items properly, something bad will happen to you or your neighbors. A key characteristic of post-traumatic stress disorder is that the individual tries to prevent trauma reminders. They also assume that if they remember what happened too vividly, they'll start to re-experience it and emotions could be stronger than they can handle. In this chapter we will discuss in effect various anxiety disorders. The techniques we talk about to manage anxiety are, however, general.

If you feel uncomfortable a lot of the time, or your anxiety is so bad that it starts affecting your daily life, you may be struggling from one of the popular anxiety disorders. Although we stated that in certain circumstances anxiety is natural, it becomes a concern when:

- It is out of proportion to the high-stress situation.

- If a stressful situation is gone, and it continues to exist.

- When there is no stressful situation and it happens for no explicable reason.

It is very normal for people who have anxiety to have depressive symptoms too. Cognitive-behavioral therapy explores how our perceptions, desires, physical feelings and behaviors work to sustain our anxiety. If we experience a "threat" of some sort –

be it a fear of something happening in the moment or a worry for something that could happen in the future – our minds and bodies respond in different ways. When we experience the physical feelings of anxiety, we think that it really implies there is a danger (even though there's not one in real life) and so we get more feelings of anxiety. This in turn contributes to enhanced physical feelings as our bodies react to our perceptions. If we are frightened of something, we avoid it normally. This in turn can make us believe that we can genuinely fear something – and we are never given the opportunity to validate our fears by avoiding it. Therefore, our fear about this situation increases. We also focus on our fears and concerns to try and feel them, keep us safe or stop bad events. This habit, however, is usually inefficient and serves simply to increase our anguish without strengthening or changing our circumstance. It may be helpful to seek reassurance from close associates, browse for the internet, or consult specialists, and it eases our anxiety in a lasting way. But, when people are anxious they tend to seek validation, feel better for a little while, and then need more reassurance. Hardly anything improves, and they never find more efficient and reliable ways to manage their anxieties.

If you are suffering from anxiety problems, you are definitely not alone. Anxiety disorders are common in today's society. One in every eight adults at some point in their lives may have suffered anxiety disorder.

There are different forms of anxiety disorder - stress reaction disorder, obsessive-compulsive disorder (OCD), phobias, post-traumatic stress disorder (PTSD), panic disorder, agoraphobia, generalized anxiety disorder (GAD), health anxiety and social anxiety disorder. They all have some common symptoms.

Below are the key areas that lead to anxiety problems. Do any of these describe your situation?

- Easily irritable or upsetting?

- Unable to relax and settle?

- Difficulty relaxing?

- Cannot stop or regulate worries?

- Worrying about pretty nearly everything?

- Tense, anxious or depressed?

- Fearing something terrible might take place?

If any regularly apply to you, it may be beneficial to see your GP to discuss what happens and what treatment is available, including using self-help books like this one.

What Is An Anxiety Disorder?

Let us review the various kinds of anxiety disorders in more detail. All of them share many common aspects. We will then research the methods used by cognitive-behavioral therapy to help individuals cope with them.

Generalized Anxiety Disorder (GAD)

Suffering from GAD implies that you can feel nervous, tense and stress over issues that others think are very trivial most of the day. When you do not fix it, the problem will last years and significantly affect your quality of life. Generalized anxiety can often be something which people feel they have always encountered to a degree - "I have always been a little bit more concerned" - but which becomes more disabled during or after periods of heightened or intense stress. Even after distressing incidents such as disappointment, redundancy or divorce, it may become extremely difficult and can start a significant duration after these incidents.

Women are much more likely than men to be hospitalized with GAD, maybe partially because women are far more likely to see their physician and confess to such feelings. You are more likely to suffer GAD if you are 35–54 years of age, whether you are separated or divorced, or if you are a single parent – but just anyone can develop this condition.

Someone with GAD typically understands that their thoughts are unreasonable and unacceptable. However, sometimes they do not even know what they are worried about – they are just uneasy and cannot sit down or relax. For a diagnosis of GAD, three or more of the following signs typically occur:

- Restlessness

- Disturbed sleep

- Irritability

- Tiredness

- Physical tension

- Problems concentrating or feeling as if your mind just goes blank.

Case study – Jane (GAD)

Jane's at the beginning of her thirties. Her young boy just began school. Jane is back at work and wants her new boss who was named during her maternity leave to be very impressed with her. She has always been a bit of a perfectionist, but she used to have time to dedicate extra hours to her overly high expectations. Now she feels it is all too difficult with the extra expectations of motherhood and work. At work, she fears that she is not as quick and effective as other colleagues who have not had a maternity break. She is as well worried about how her kid copes, thinking that she should be a full-time mother, but recognizing that her income is necessary to be able to fulfill her needs. There's no harmony at homework-related thoughts interfere continuously, as do self-critical opinions about her capacity both as a wife and a mother. She has a full house for GAD symptoms! Constant restlessness and worry, sleeping difficulties, physical discomfort and many aches and pains.

Post-Traumatic Stress Disorder

When people suffer a trauma like a car accident or are assaulted or robbed at gunpoint. Fear, repetitive and distressing opinions and remembrances of the event, a feeling of emotional numbness, distance from those around them and intense anxiety are all very common. You can also try avoiding any recalls or repercussions of the event. These side effects are all very natural and are part of the process to conform and understand what happened. Such symptoms usually reduce in just a few weeks after a trauma and most people recuperate well with time and support. To others, though, these effects continue or even intensify over time, and what happened does not seem possible to move on from. In some cases, symptoms can persist or unexpectedly start months or years after the trauma. This is called post-traumatic stress disorder. We are going to address this and recommend ways to deal with it later, which deals with the use of cognitive-behavioral therapy to cope with stressful life events.

Phobias

A phobia is a deep fear or anxiety that is beyond the control of the situation that triggers it. Getting close to or in touch with the scary object or circumstance induces anxiety. And just the thought of what you are phobic about is upsetting and troubling. Sometimes you can escape the situation that is feared, but in other cases it can hinder your life. Moreover, the more you try to avoid it, the more you keep trying to avoid it and over time, it becomes more and more limiting.

There are also phobia to particular objects or circumstances. Claustrophobia (fear of enclosed or cramped space), fears of particular animals and fears of needles, choking or vomiting, are some common ones. There are hundreds of phobia, but they are all handled according to the same grade exposure rules, which we are going to address later in this chapter.

Social Phobia

Social phobia or social anxiety disorder may be the most prevalent phobia. You are really worried with what others might think of you or how they might judge you. You are afraid to meet or "perform" before others, most especially strangers. You are afraid you are going to be humiliating and that people are going to think you are dumb, incompetent, underprivileged, reckless or even crazy. You stop circumstances of this nature as much as possible. It is really extremely difficult to psyche-up yourself up to go anywhere – you sometimes leave invites open until the last minute, not wanting to involve yourself. You are also very nervous and depressed while you are in the frightening situation and might well leave early. Like all anxiety issues, it is important to combine positive thought and behavioral interventions in order to resolve social phobia.

Panic Disorder

Recurring panic attacks occur in people with panic disorder. A panic attack is a serious attack of fear and anxiety that unexpectedly happens, sometimes without warning and with no obvious cause. The side effects of anxiety during a panic attack can be extreme, and include: heart-pounding, shiver, respiratory distress, chest pain, faintness, numbness or pins and needles. Each panic attack typically takes 5-10 minutes, but sometimes it lasts up to two hours in waves. Heart attacks are extremely terrifying occurrences and people will sometimes feel like they are dying when they happen. This inevitably leads to the fear – to the fear that an attack will take place and this time something terrible may happen. People seek to cope through avoidance, being fearful of any situation where they think an attack can occur or where they may not be able to escape the panic attack. This can seriously restrict someone is life and for other people agoraphobia, which is soon identified, is also related.

Agoraphobia

Agoraphobia literally means 'fear of market place' in ancient Greek. The word refers to fear of open spaces and often includes problems of being in the public – public transport, shops, crossing bridges, crowds or even just being away from their home. This is generally difficult, if not impossible, to do this alone, even though some people who suffer from agoraphobia can do it alone if they are supported by someone they respect and trust.

All of the problems causing agoraphobia for people are unified by a basic fear - that there is no support in a situation where you are overloaded with panic, and you will find it hard, if not impossible, to flee to a safe place (normally your home).

You get highly nervous and depressed when you are in a frightening position and have an overwhelming urge to flee. Many people with agoraphobia stay in their homes for much or all of the time to avoid this fear and panic. Unfortunately, however, they will have panic attacks even in their homes and hence believe they must always have somebody with them.

Approximately 5 % of the population suffer from agoraphobia and panic disorder, it affects women more than men and frequently encountered between the ages of 25 and 35. Agoraphobia impacts up to one-third of panic-disorder patients and occurs before an attack starts. The fear means that a person is attempting to avoid areas where panic attacks are likely to occur and, while avoidance may help in holding panic attacks in check, life-restraints usually only tend to escalate and affect both the individual and those in their neighborhood.

Case Study – Billy (Panic Disorder With Agoraphobia)

Billy is a 25-year-old employee. He travels by public transport every day. He likes to journey by train. It gave him opportunity to read the newspaper and relax before the beginning of a stressful day. But one day the train was notably crowded. It was quite hot and the air-conditioning system of the train had crashed and burned. Billy began to feel warm. He discovered that he was sweating profusely and his heart immediately started to race. His chest hurt and he felt unsteady. Something must be very completely mistaken, he thought. He was persuaded that he had a heart attack. At the next stop, he got off the train and called emergency services. In A&E he was tested and told that his heart was working well. He had just experienced a panic attack. He felt soothed but shaken and afraid of what had actually occurred. He did feel like he was going to die. Never again did he want to feel like that. He was very nervous the next time he was on the train and again he started to experience symptoms. Again, he concentrated on them and felt the fearsome feeling that he was dying. It was very difficult to come to terms with the feelings and he had to exit the train and go home. Progressively, Billy found that his fear of the signs of panic is causing him to avoid more and more circumstances where he felt the panic attack might happen again and he was frightened that he may not be lucky to escape.

Over time, the avoidance of Billy became more and more established. He did not believe he was able to resist the signs of panic, so he just did not do anything he thought could cause them. He gave up his job and began working from home. He slowly declined and his social life decreased. As he avoided further circumstances, his anxiety that a disastrous attack would occur increased and he felt gradually unable to break free.

Obsessive-Compulsive Disorder (OCD)

Obsessive-compulsive disorder includes repeated obsessions, compulsions or the two. Obsessions are frequently occurring invasive, unwelcomed and undesired urges, thoughts or images that end up causing you to feel nervous or disgusted. Popular obsessive-compulsive disorders are concerns of getting infected by soil, germs, illnesses or body fluids and also fears of disasters. They can include fears about abuse that will come to you or harm you will cause other people, even though it is against your volition, like bestiality and pedophilia. Fears concerning religious convictions are also popular.

Compulsions are thoughts or acts that you believe you have to push yourself to do or have, and almost always feel that you have to replicate it until you get it right. A compulsion is primarily a response to the anxiety triggered by an obsession. Persistent hand washing in response to excessive fear of dirt or germs is a common example. A person may overwhelmingly afraid that they can get harmful germs on their palms just from touching different things and that these could be dangerous to themselves or human beings around them. Therefore, they might feel compelled to wash or sanitize their hands very often to minimize this fear. Others compulsions include repeated mopping, checking, counting, touching, placing objects in specific positions and also storing objects.

Professional assistance is often necessary, because it may

initially be difficult for an individual to distinguish between obsessional thought and real danger. Likewise, if you believe that you will hurt others against your will, you would naturally not be willing to test it just in case you get to know it was real.

OCD patients often have an overblown sense of responsibility. It may be their primary responsibility to protect themselves against the hazards of the world, which they usually exaggerate significantly. You may also feel like you have to ensure that there is no harm to anyone. The execution of a ritual or compulsion very often does not solve the issue. They may have irrational thoughts about danger coming to others. They might then feel, for instance, that they have to remove stones from the pavements to prevent anybody from tripping but then feel worried that the location they have moved the stone to may hurt someone instead.

Health Anxiety

Some health issues can be helpful, as it implies that you can seek to maintain a healthier lifestyle.. People who have had health issues, in general and especially a heart attack or cancer, frequently assume that something bad will take place next time, unless they make some adjustments. Although this attitude can be very beneficial to some, others may become extremely obsessed with their wellbeing. Many people find that this heightened anxiety occurs after the sickness of someone they know, after a major life-changing event or just out of the ordinary, for no apparent cause. Any insignificant symptom is completely blown out of dimension. A mild sniffle is an inevitable death attributed to swine flu, a swelling on the skin tends to mean cancerous growth, exhaustion is multiple sclerosis, while headaches are a brain tumor - which is of course won't be incurable. People with health anxiety frequently visit their doctor and will eventually carry out multiple examinations, tests and appointments to specialists that often amount to nothing. They can also spend a great deal of time online and in books researching a disease. Concern and worry about diseases can take people's lives and cause tremendous suffering.

How CBT Can Help With Anxiety

The good news is that cognitive-behavioral therapy practitioners have developed multiple validated strategies to help people conquer anxiety disorders. The following approaches can be used for a number of the above-described disorders. Some are more effective than others in some cases. Check it out and see what work is going on for you. We will first discuss how you cope with your thoughts and then analyze some coping approaches that can better control the anxieties.

Thought Balancing

This technique is essential to cognitive therapy and involves a different analysis of your anxious thoughts. You will now start to see that feelings are just emotions and that they are not really true. Thoughts should be seen merely as mental events. However, we sometimes react to them as if they were factual statements rather than suggestions or ideas. Just because you think something terrible is going to occur doesn't mean that it is guaranteed? Some thoughts will be real, some will not and between these two extremes will be a broad grey area. Keeping this in mind is a great starting point.

Challenge Perfectionism

Do you always demand more from yourself than you can actually accomplish? Do you have much higher judging standards for yourself than for others? If that is so, then you can fall into self-defeating habits that keep you depressed and very frustrated.

Be careful of "always," "should" and "must" when you talk to yourself - these words are hardly helpful. Try to adhere to the 'good enough is good enough' rule. You can still be good at certain things, but it is much more likely to achieve results if you seek excellence instead of perfection. Do you know someone who is great in all respects? No? So how come do you actually think you can achieve this?

Examine Your Beliefs About Worry

Apparently, a lot of people find worry to be a big issue because of the opinions they hold about the procedure of worry. Some people have optimistic beliefs about worry and they include:

- Worrying helps me organize myself even more.

- Worrying helps to stop terrible things and helps me to remain safe.

- If I did not worry frequently, I would always get stuffs wrong.

At the same time, they may have adverse convictions about worry like:

- Worrying could drive me crazy.

- Worrying will make me sick.

- Worrying puts pressure on my heart.

For convictions like these it is not surprising that some people find it difficult not to worry – and instead feel very afraid because they are not able to stop.

Now try to think critically about them. When we are worried, we consciously try to predict every negative thing that might happen to prevent it (somehow). But is this simply possible? Is it not true that bad occurrences happen sometimes, regardless of how much we knew beforehand? Is it really possible for us to make things happen or not happen with our thought processes? Time we expend on it does not help us to become more coordinated or more effective. The effect of worry is typically just some more tension, stress and anxiety. Research has shown that stress can physically affect us. However, there is very little proof that stress and worry individually (in the absence of underlying medical problems) may cause us permanent or devastating physical harm. Worry would probably not affect your physical or mental health. What we can promise, though, is that worry leaves you miserable and devoid of life - all the more reason to focus on getting rid of it.

Absorbing Yourself In Something Else

Psychologists can easily tell you to 'distract or draw away yourself' when you are worrying too much or in the midst of a panic attack – but in reality, it is very challenging to do this. Dissatisfaction with this is very normal. Our mind is a very busy environment – and it is built that way. We encounter countless thoughts in a day, and it can be very difficult to ignore the emotionally challenging ones like our worries. Nonetheless, we know that you will learn to move on with practice and self-restraint rather than remain trapped with them. And telling yourself not to worry is definitely not going to help. Be firm and gentle with yourself and your active mind. Once you have passed through the worry tree and have recognized that you have done everything you can, remember that any further worry is unfruitful. Do not be annoyed - just calmly turn your attention to something else that absorbs. Choose an activity that effectively holds your attention and concentrates all your five senses on this activity. You can prefer to talk to a friend or relative, watch a TV or do a homework or physical activity. Whatever it may be, concentrate all your attention on it. Your mind is going to try to meddle with worries, but every time it does that remind it that it is not beneficial and get your attention back to what you were doing. You might have to do this a lot at first, and that can be challenging. Do not give up or tell yourself that you cannot - that is only going to sabotage your great work. Nobody understands this immediately. It takes a lot of training, but it gets easier over time.

Believe it or not, being able to sit back and relax is a skill that many of us have, unfortunately, never mastered sufficiently. Day in and day out, as we are busy running from one job to another, we quite often find that we have a lot of muscle tension. Have you ever found your arms, neck and back aching you at the end of a very long or exhausting day? Most of this may be due to tension in the muscles. The tension rises as we are nervous, worried or anxious which can lead to headache, fatigue and tiredness. Learning to physically relax can be a valuable investment to help you handle anxiety or stress better. It takes practice just like learning any other skill. When you are learning, the following activities should be repeated every day. Setting aside some time each day for a workout often allows you to establish the best practice of prioritizing a short duration for everyday relaxation. When you eventually learn how to relax, uphold this habit – it can make a huge difference to find time to relax every day.

Exercise 1: Deep Muscle Relaxation

- Choose a safe and convenient spot, where no one will be able to bother you. Choose a time of day when you will most likely feel relaxed.

- Lie down, feel at ease and shut your eyes.

- Focus for a few minutes on your breathing. Try to breathe calmly and quietly, count 'in-2-3, out-2-3.'

- You are now going to work through various muscle groups and learn to tense first, then to relax. You should breathe in as you tense and breathe out as you relax.

- Begin with your hands. Clench one hand firmly at first. Remember the tension that this creates in your hand and forearm muscles.

- Pay attention to the tension and relax your hand for some seconds. Note the distinction between the relaxation and the tension. You may feel a burning sensation. This is the relaxation starting to build up.

- Do the same with the second hand now.

- Every time you relax a group of muscles, think about how they feel when relaxed. Try not to relax, just let the tension go. Let the muscles relax as much as possible.

- Concentrate on the difference between the way you feel when you are relaxed and tensed.

- Now do the same thing with the other body muscle groups. Tense them for a couple of seconds, and then relax. Pay attention to how they feel, and then just let the tension go. It is important to maintain the same order as practice in the muscle groups.

- Hands - first clench and then relax.

- Arms - try and bend your elbow and then tense your arms. You will feel the tension particularly in your upper arms. Keep in mind to do this for some seconds and then relax.

- Neck - press the back of the head and move it slowly from side to side. Pay attention to how the tension is moving.

Then put your head forward in a stable position.

- Face - there are a lot of muscles around the face, but mostly focus on your jaw and forehead. Draw your eyebrows down into a frown. Relax your forehead. You can as well raise your eyebrows and relax. Clench your jaw now and then relax – see the difference.

- Chest - take a very deep breath, hold on to it for some seconds. Allow your breathing to go back to normal.

- Stomach - tense the muscles of the stomach as close as possible and then relax.

- Buttocks - tense the muscles of the buttocks and relax.

- Legs - try and straighten your legs, bend your feet in a way that it is pointed towards our face and then relax. Leave the toes wiggling.

It could be helpful for you to get a buddy to read the directions to you. Do not try too hard when you go through the exercise – just let it unfold.

Exercise 2: A New Take On 'Bibliotherapy'

- This is not about reading a book – it is about using one! You are just going to need 15 minutes, but if you want to do something longer, enjoy!

- Choose a relatively large book, take it in a quiet spot, and then set your alarm to 15 minutes, that way you do not have to worry about the time.

- Lie on your back, open the book, and put it on your belly facing down.

- Focus on breathing in steadily via your nose for a total of 4 seconds, hold your breath for 2 slow seconds, then breathe out steadily via your mouth for 4 more seconds. Continue to repeat this process.

- Still keep your attention on the book. Watch as it goes up and down with the movement of your belly. Pay attention to it as closely as possible.

- The busy mind will continue to interfere with other distracting thoughts. Do not pursue them, but tell yourself that you will handle them later, as you are doing your bibliotherapy at the moment.

Then go back to focusing on counting, breathing, and watching the book rising and falling ... is that the alarm ringing already?

Exercise 3: A Safe Place

This is a type of visualization exercise that would require some training to fully understand it. It is also known as self-hypnosis.

People always assume that they are not great at visualization, but most of us can actually create images in our minds with practice, patience and perseverance. The good news is that study shows that you do not have to take vibrant images for this to be able to work – blurry, fugitive ones are just as great.

- Find a suitable room and comfortably sit or lie down. Again, it would help to set the alarm for 15 minutes so that you do not have to worry about the time.

- Relax and focus on your breathing. Breathe in and out of your stomach slowly and intensely. Seek to slow down your breath to about 10-12 breaths a minute, but then you can ignore that. Just breathe as it comes.

- Shut your eyes and begin to imagine yourself in a comfortable, warm and peaceful environment. It might be a tropical beach, a summer park, your bed or on the moon - it could be anywhere. It can be either real or imaginary.

- Concentrate on your senses. What can you see, hear, feel, taste and touch in this peaceful environment? How do you feel when you are here? What can you find around you?

- Explore your peaceful environment for a few minutes. Relax your muscles and allow all the tension go away while you are peaceful environment.

- Your busy mind will again attempt to confuse you with

other ideas, questions or images. Just let them go gently. Keep in mind that you are in your safe environment at the moment - other thoughts can be addressed later. Exercise turning your thoughts down - just like you turn the volume of a radio down.

With training, you can find that when you are stressed or anxious, you can very easily and accurately call your safe spot. Going to this place briefly may help you to refocus your mind, calm down and then move into a less stressed state of mind.

Break The Panic Cycle

We looked earlier at how physical thoughts and sensations communicate directly to develop a panic attack. The first course of action is to better inform yourself about the triggers of panic attacks. Panic feels unbelievably terrible – horrible. It is really difficult to accept that you should not encounter anything tragic. We realize, however, that panic is a self-limiting mechanism. It cannot hurt you. There is no proof that anybody has ever passed away from a panic attack without an underlying medical condition. There is no proof that anyone has ever "gone crazy" because of a panic attack. Just because you feel very strong physical feelings does not necessarily mean that your devastation is unavoidable. The odds are that it will not happen at all.

For instance, a lot of people feel that they will pass out when they have a panic attack. But do you know what must happen to your blood pressure before you can pass out? It must fall unexpectedly. What do you think normally happens to your blood pressure when you experience a panic attack? It increases (but not dangerously). The only exception is if you have a blood phobia or injury, in which case it may reduce your blood pressure when you see these things. Thus, it's practically impossible for anyone to pass out during a panic attack.

Take into account what your fears are when you panic:

- What's the worst thing that could possibly happen?

- How likely is it to actually happen (instead of how much it feels like it will)?

- How likely would anyone else believe it to be?

- If the worst actually happened, how almost certain is it that you would not be capable of dealing with it (no matter how terrible it was)?

It can be very helpful to think this way when attempting to break a panic loop. Ultimately, however, the only way to show yourself that all this is true is to face your concerns and experiment this truly innovative way of looking at things. The following parts on graded exposure and behavioral experiments will help.

Graded Exposure

Exposure therapy is the approach that cognitive-behavioral therapy uses to help people confront their fears and conquer them. It is used in various ways to treat all anxiety disorders. Here we define the basic concepts that apply to all of them.

<u>Develop a graded hierarchy</u>. Write 1 to 10 on the side of a sheet of paper. 1 is an operation which is not especially scary - something you might be a little worried about but could do by giving yourself an extra push. 10 represents the most frightening behaviors for you - those which make you say: "No way! I would never do that!' Start by writing down something for the top and bottom scale. Then imagine what could happen in the middle - what would be the 5? Keep going until you have 10 different activities and the scale is fulfilled. It can be helpful to get support from someone who knows you well.

<u>Start working through your ladder from the bottom up</u>. You may consider telling someone near you to accompany you if that will help you get started, but then it is very necessary that you train on your own. Continue to repeat each item on your list until you feel comfortable about it and until you notice that whatever you were afraid of (bats entangled in your hair, spiders crawling around you, falling down from a height or perhaps even drowning), does not happen. Take note of what you did learn at each phase of the exercise and use it to help yourself advance to the next step. Keep in mind to compliment

yourself on each move, rather than thinking 'it is simple for some people so my accomplishments are not significant.' For you, these are great achievements.

<u>Remain in the situation until your anxiety falls</u>. Score your anxiety out of 10 at the initial stages of each exposure task. It is probably going to be very high at first. It is also very key to remain in the circumstance until your anxiety falls to at least half of what it was initially. This can be difficult. When you 'escape' too early, though, you will not figure out how to cope with your anxiety. Remain in the situation - the anxiety will fall and you will know what you need to move forward.

Activity Scheduling And Planning

Quite often we feel nervous and frightened because we have taken on too much than we can handle or did not effectively plan our time. Effective preparation is a critical skill all of us have to work on.

We often get anxious when we do a lot and the anxiety can cripple us - so that we cannot deal with all the things that we have to do. We can obey certain rules to prevent us from getting frustrated and trapped in this way.

1. Be A Hummingbird Than A Butterfly

Watch a butterfly. It begins to flutter from one location to another, and when it decides to stop, you won't really see it doing anything until it starts flying again. If we are anxious, we tend to behave like this butterfly - to jump from one task to another, trying to take on more than we can handle and ultimately doing nothing effectively or fully. On the other hand, a hummingbird stays in one place, hovering even with the pull of gravity, sipping the nectar from one flower before moving to the next flower. The principle is to do one task at a time, however much you need to do, and concentrate solely on that one thing until it is completed and you can move on.

2. Break Things Down Into Manageable Steps

Have you ever seen everything you have to do and felt exhausted, not having any idea of where to begin? It is so enticing to give up any effort to start your task and just hide your head in the sand. Rather than doing that, divide tasks into smaller steps. What should be the first thing to do? Then do the first task without having to worry about the next one. Now proceed to the next tiny step and you will have accomplished a colossal mission before you know. Do it for only five minutes if something feels too daunting. Do not think any more ahead.

3. Write Out An Activity Plan

List the things you plan to do every day. 'Make sure your options are practical (this possibly means you'll have to cross out some tasks), and prioritize them. What needs to be done today? Who could wait a little? Make the decision of which task you want to do, when and how long to spend on every task. And add a little extra time for good measure. Draw up the day's timetable. Put in the organic breaks (tea and coffee, meals and toilet stops) and even allow quick day-dreaming times! Then obey your time schedule. As you work, imagine yourself as a hummingbird and float continuously until the task is done, then just go to the next one.

4. Problem Solve

If you are not aware of how to handle some certain task, take some time to work it out rather than to panic. Are there any support sources you can use? Who could help? When you are trapped, there is no shame in asking for assistance - or how else can anyone know anything? What else would anyone else say about this?

5. Write down the concern explicitly

Now spend a little time coming up with ideas of every possible answer. Go for it - imagine as many as you can and write them down. Go through every solution and identify the benefits and drawbacks. Write them down and give any answer a mark out of 10 after weighing the advantages and disadvantages. Then pick the solution with the best scores. You might even get a buddy to assist you in this task. Not all problems have an immediate fix, but breaking stuff down into smaller pieces often can help us see first, or figure out what information we need to collect in order to find a solution. Eventually, test out the solution. Did it work? Otherwise, why not? Go back to your list and try something else.

Chapter 4 - Anger Management And CBT

Most people are occasionally angry when their personal standards, expectations, rules or values are jeopardized, compromised or infringed. Anger can be regarded as an emotional reaction to a perceived threat or danger, and transient anger is part of the normal emotional range in this regard. Anger can be a suitable emotional response to frustration, injuries, insults or threats to survival or psychological integrity.

However, angry feelings differ from anger problems. If anger is automatic, difficult to control, protracted, disproportionate and destructive, it can signal the underlying problem of anger or an anger disorder. Anger issues can occur when intermittent emotions of frustration linger and shift to indignation, hostility, hate and disruptive fury.

Psychologically, socially and physiologically, anger problems may be damaging. Anger will increase the direct danger of physical violence and harm our working lives, relationships and physical health. Unchecked anger can negatively influence your work, your health and your relationships. Anger can take your life and lead to suicide, depression and violence. Uncontrolled outbursts and erratic behavior may also put your children, neighbors and coworkers in danger. If you have anger issues, it is imperative that you get the support you need to establish functional management strategies.

Anger is a completely natural and balanced emotion, which we all feel periodically. Mild anger with a feeling of rage generally represents the situation in which we believe we have been violated or disappointed. However, in retrospect, we all know that occasionally our tolerance for incidents can be too high to affect us normally. When we experience persistent and uncontrollable anger frequently, it begins to have a negative effect on our lives and our mental wellbeing.

Understanding our anger can be the key to controlling our feelings and to ensuring that we process them positively. Anger is always triggered when we evaluate circumstances that we have been:

- Unequal or unfairly treated

- Frustrated

- Attacked

- Blindsided

- Deceived

Anger may be positive in certain circumstances and drive us to respond in cases that we would not have before. It can lead to healthy competition, force us to defend people we love and inspire us to fight for a cause or for a wrongdoing.

When tackling our anger issues, cognitive-behavioral therapy is allows us to assess which situation we have to respond and which responses are highly sensitive. When it is reasonable to be angry, cognitive-behavioral therapy teaches us a better way to communicate our emotions in a healthier manner-to make our anger more constructive. Anger usually is a concern when it interferes with our ability to sustain relationships, conducts our everyday tasks or becomes detrimental to us or others. But when the anger is unhelpful, how do you know?

Anger explosions may be demonstrated in various ways but in general, unhelpful anger takes three forms:

1) External aggression and violence - Shouting, being physically violent to others, verbal abuse or hurling of objects.

2) Internal aggression and violence - Self-harm, dispossessing yourself of essential human needs like food or things that bring happiness, negative self-talk.

3) Non-violent passive-aggressive behavior - Disregarding others or avoiding constructive communication, undermining other people chance of success or using sarcasm in an effort to escape substantive conversations.

Mistaken Assumptions Angry People Often Make

<u>They can't help it</u>. Angry people come up with lots of justifications. Women are going to blame their PMS. Both males and females will blame their worries, their stress, or their exhaustion. This doesn't understand that many people who are worried or exhausted or stressed over PMS don't come lashing out at the world. Angry people also do not understand that they are literally giving themselves the approval to rant. They have a great deal of influence in that regard.

<u>The only way to express anger is to lash out</u>. Those who are get angry claim that the anger is like a surge in steam in an overly hot steam engine. They think they have to blow off the steam to be all right. Ultimately, raging just creates more of the same thing.

<u>Frustration is intolerable</u>. Angry individuals cannot sit with fear, anxiety or frustration. These feelings to them are an indicator that they are being called into question. If life does not go in their direction, if somebody does not see things from their point of view, whether they contradict their best intentions or make an equivocation, they absolutely cannot accept them. To them, lashing out is better than being stuck with these feelings. They don't understand that anger is a common part of life for everyone and that it is also a source of inspiration and

innovation.

<u>It's more critical to win than to be right</u>. Severely angry people also assume that when conflict happens, their reputation will be at stake. They take it too seriously when challenged. They suffer a loss of self-esteem when they are losing an argument. At that time, even if you are wrong, they tend to find a need to affirm their authority. They will find a way to demonstrate that the other person is totally incorrect when they are certain that they are the one wrong. For rational human beings, self-esteem is founded on the ability to set ego aside, in attempt to find the best workable alternative.

<u>"Respect" implies that people do things their way</u>. When another car drive too closely behind, when a partner fails to follow through with a plan, when a child does not move when asked to do something, they feel humiliated. Disrespect or humiliation is unacceptable to them. Causing a lot of commotion and trying to intimidate is their way of legitimizing their right to "respect" by anyone. Unfortunately, if fear is the basis for "respect," it negatively impacts love and caring.

<u>The way to make things right is to fight</u>. Many angry people got to learn at a master's feet. It's their "part of nature" having been brought up by parents who fight all the time. They have no idea how to resolve disputes or how to manage disagreements except by spiraling out of control. And then they become more like the parent they despised and hated when they were young.

Others should fully comprehend that when they were angry, they didn't necessarily mean what they did or said. Angry people actually think that anger bestows them the right to go on a rampage. It is up to others not to take things they have done or said seriously. They say they were only angry after all. They fail to actually realize that others are genuinely embarrassed, hurt, humiliated or terrified.

How Can CBT Help With My Anger?

Cognitive-behavioral therapy teaches us that when we're upset, our actions depends on how we handle our emotions and convey our emotions. In particular, cognitive behavior therapy is indeed the perfect way to help overcome your anger problems.

Cognitive-behavioral therapy should be a process of collaboration between your therapist and you. That is the reason why you have work with your therapist to recognize your own personal sources of rage when you decide to get cognitive-behavioral therapy. You will also learn how the negative thoughts and behavioral patterns can alter your feelings of anger.

Your sessions will provide you with the resources and coping strategies required to ensure that healthy cognitive habits are formed. Cognitive-behavioral therapy also shows you how to take a more positive approach to thought. We have assembled some of the major ways in which cognitive-behavioral therapy tends to help with anger problems:

1. Helps you detect the causes and circumstances that trigger an angry response - Everybody has different triggers when it comes to anger. Some people are triggered by the thought of being denigrated, while other people are outraged when they feel disgraced or derided. Regardless of whatever causes your anger, cognitive-behavioral therapy will help you better understand why you respond the way you do when you begin to feel irritated. Cognitive-behavioral therapy can also help you predict circumstances where you can get upset and teach you innovative approaches for behavior and thinking.

2. It teaches you new coping strategies to discourage angry reactions - After you have established some of your main triggers, your therapist will propose new solutions to address your impulsivity, anger and frustration. A few of these frustrations might include learning to acknowledge that some are part of everyday life.

3. It provides you with new techniques of emotional management to handle angry feelings - We cannot drastically alter our feelings but one thing cognitive-behavioral therapy tells us is that we can control them by working actively to develop our thoughts and behavior.

When we get angry, we become too sensitive to situations and even distorted at times. However, we can learn to create more realistic perceptions by adopting certain cognitive restructuring techniques. Next time you get angry and think "everything is lost," consider replacing that thought with "even though this is frustrating that this has actually occurred, it is not the end of the road." Cognitive-behavioral therapy allows us to learn about how to maintain our composure in helpful and practical circumstances.

Chapter 5 - Beating Bad Habits And Building Better Ones

It is a common saying that practice makes you perfect. When we conscientiously keep repeating an activity, it can be to enhance our skill and get to where we can do it with little thought. Habits are things that we do on a regular basis, often with no thought. This ability, with minimal conscious thinking or control, to do things almost autopilotly is very essential to our way of life.

Consider skills you have learned - imagine trying to climb up a staircase, tie your boot laces or drive a car when you had to think and plan every step of the way every time you did it. To learn a new, complicated skill such as driving is really difficult at first and requires a serious amount of concentration. You must think about every stage and may feel overpowered with the number of things you must do all at once. However, once you have established the skill, you will not have to think of each step anymore – you can do it automatically and free yourself to focus on other things like where you intend to go, or trying to avoid your neighbor's cat running into the road.

Similarly, it is very useful to develop habits. For example, you are well-positioned on developing the habit of cleanliness if you conscientiously put your clothes in your laundry basket after you undress instead of putting it on the floor and you consciously make sure that that you return objects back to where you took them after use. The main disadvantage to this is that we can also develop certain habits that are not so helpful. There are several different kinds of "bad" habits that may be bad in numerous ways. Many refer to the way we manage and treat our bodies – such as using dangerous substances, eating unhealthy foods, not drinking sufficient water or doing too little workout. We might pick at our skin, bite our nails or pull our hair out. Others could be interpersonal habits. Think about how you deal with other people for a moment. Are you extremely deprecatory? Do you displease your partner by being inconsiderate or insensitive about certain things around the house? Perhaps you are always late or disorganized. These include behavior patterns that can become common practice. The bad news is that effort is needed to change these patterns. The excellent thing is that it can be achieved, often with tremendous success.

A Word About Addiction

A variety of techniques discussed in this chapter are effective for transforming or changing all forms of habits, which involve addictive substances including nicotine (which can be found in all types of tobacco), alcohol and other drugs. That being said, substance abuse can be more than just a habit. It may cause addiction and you may require additional assistance to give it up, other than learning how to modify your habit.

There are different available ways of obtaining nicotine apart from via tobacco. Many individuals find it much easier to stop the habit of tobacco by having nicotine at the beginning, for instance with patches and chewing gum. They then minimize their consumption of nicotine, slowly withdraw from the medicine, and break their smoking addiction or any other kind of tobacco abuse. If you wish to quit taking tobacco, you can first test the options that we offer and not ingest nicotine in a different form, to assess whether you actually have to quit the nicotine slowly. The negative impacts of nicotine addiction are normally pretty short-lived and physical hankering will stop within a few days - it is then the habit of using tobacco needs to be broken.

Understand that any drug usage in the early stages can be extremely difficult to change. You have both addiction and habits to break away - and you have to do so to the point when you are less convinced of your ability to get things done. Withdrawal from alcohol or other drugs addiction can be extremely challenging that some people need professional guidance with the process. Consider visiting your doctor or a specialist in addiction issues. There are numerous sources of assistance out there. If you therefore find it almost impossible to quit taking a substance using only the strategies outlined in this chapter, please go and seek for professional assistance. As soon as your physical addiction to a drug is resolved, you will then be able to focus on overcoming the behavioral and cognitive patterns you developed around your addiction.

How can I tell if I'm drinking too much?

A large percentage of people know that alcohol abuse is a major issue but it is incredibly hard for them or others to acknowledge it. It is imperative to make sure that you don't regularly drink more than the approved number of units for your gender, but so is keeping your drinking behavior in check. 1 out of every 25 adults in the United States is estimated to be addicted to alcohol.

Answer the questions below. Make sure you're transparent - it's confidential to you, and can bring to light whether you should really do something about your drinking habit:

1. You find it very difficult to give up drinking?

2. Avoid activities or occasions where you know you will not have access to a drink?

3. Do you sometimes feel you must have a drink to cope with certain circumstances?

4. Do you on regular basis do stuff whilst drinking that you feel bad about when sober?

5. Do you find it extremely difficult to go for 'half-glass' or to adhere to a glass of wine?

6. Do you always like to drink alone?

7. Do you or anybody you know have to consciously set a limit on your drinking?

8. Do you get physical symptoms when you try to stay away from alcohol?

9. Has anybody ever raised concerns about your drinking habit?

10. Do you often drink when exhausted or stressed?

11. Do you normally drink as a way of getting rid of a crapulence or hangover?

If you replied with a 'yes' to any of these queries, you may have an alcohol problem. If you believe you fall into this group then I suggest that you get your doctor's advice.

Step 1: Deciding To Change

Habits are not easy to change. There is a valid reason for this, as we have seen. They need to be resolute and very resilient, so that we can do things automatically. That being said, this implies that even though we try to change our habit, if we are not on our guard, it will be so easy to get back into our old habits. To make and maintain a difficult change, we have to be stimulated – if we are not stimulated or motivated then we will never be able to do the hard work that is expected of us.

Taking time to think and to evaluate your motivation to improve your behavior would increase your chances of success. Ensure that you come up with the advantages (pros) and costs (cons) of choosing to remain the same and of changing your habit - they are very often direct opposites of each other but not all the time. If you leave out a segment you might very well miss out on a key factor in helping you make a change. The smiley faces are from these segments that hold the reasons that most definitely inspire you to change. , then you are much more likely to make that change. Do some work on this – ask others what they honestly think about you because they can identify certain areas you have not considered.

Of course, what will make you feel driven to change won't be based upon getting many things written in the "advantages of changing" and "cost of remaining the same" boxes. The weight of each thing also counts. You might just have a single advantage to remaining the same, but if this is something very essential to you, it will be difficult to change regardless of how much you have in all the other boxes. Just think about the weight of every pro and con identified. Can you change them in some ways? What details do you need to collect to increase the weight of the items that will help you break this habit?

Step 2: Know Your Enemy

Habits are instinctual or impulsive - it means we do not think of them, and mostly do not know why we do them or what triggers them. Take nail-biting as an example, a lot of people perform this act when they are worried or stressed, while others do it because they are distracted or bored.

You need to answer the following to be able to break a habit:

- When do you do it?

- How often?

- What are the triggers?

<u>Becoming More Aware</u> - 'Autopilot' is a mental configuration which is sometimes very useful. But when you attempt to change a habit it will become the enemy. By teaching ourselves to become more conscious of our habits, we can learn to switch between 'manual' and 'autopilot.' It needs time and practice.

Key tips:

- Remind yourself on a regular basis to be in control of

your habit.

- Write yourself a note, and pin it somewhere you will be able to see it on a regular basis.

- Tell people around you to remind you.

- Write down anything else that can help you to raise awareness.

<u>Keep A Habit Diary</u> - Another effective way of raising your awareness is to keep a habit diary. Monitor yourself every day as you carry on your routines and what happens at that moment. Look out for any form of temptation that makes you engage in the habit, and remember to put it into writing anytime you actually carry it out. You should remember any triggers that have caused it – what were you feeling, thinking, or doing when it happened? All this knowledge will allow you to get an understanding of how your behaviors are and the times or circumstances that you need to be especially careful about when contemplating a change in your habit. You can also add anything that may seem to be valuable information in your diary. The essential thing is to make notes whenever you catch yourself getting caught up in your habit. It could take some preparation and discipline because, as we know, some habits may take place without you being aware. See how many times you can catch yourself at it again.

Any kind of self-monitoring always changes everything we

attempt to measure. For instance, have you ever attempted to keep a food diary or write down all your expenses in a week? If so, you may have noticed that you adjust what you eat or spend because you always have the diary at the back of your mind. Take this into account when you try to learn more about how and when you lose yourself in the habits.

<u>Get Another Perspective</u> - When you want to learn more about your habits, it can be useful to incorporate the opinions of people around you. If you feel at ease, ask people around you what they have observed about your habit and their opinions about what precipitates it. They may have observed things that you didn't come to your mind! Their opinions will also help when you begin to break your habits actively.

Step 3: Changing Your Habit

All right, you are fully prepared to make your change now. You can be guided by using the following techniques. Be systematic about how you handle your habits. Be tenacious. You probably would find it very useful to draw up a detailed plan for how you are going to do it.

A – A Single Step At A Time

How many of us have entered into an "organization drive" or "health-kick" where we permanently attempt to alter all our habits at once? And is that approach always successful? Quite rarely. The reason so many New Year's resolutions are going awry is most probably because people are trying to change too much. Just be focused on changing one habit at a time. It takes time and hard work to adjust even a small habit – try to change a lot of things at once and the possibilities are you will not be successful with any of them.

Sometimes taking a single step at a time can as well translate to breaking down a habit into smaller components, and then changing each component one after the other. Deliberate over changing things gradually – for example, a lot of people find it easier to cut back on smoking or eating some foods until they are able to get rid of the habit entirely. Whichever way you decide to go about it - give it a thought and draw up a clear plan for yourself of how you are going to go about things. Starting off small can be beneficial. For instance, if you intend on increasing the amount of water you drink, begin by drinking one glass a day, at the same time every day. Keep it up for a couple of days then throw in one more, and so on. Do not try to drink 8 glasses a day from the beginning.

B – Be Realistic

We could all possibly do with being physically fit, more forbearing, more coordinated and incorporating many other such changes. Everybody has habits which may not be perfect. As much as trying to improve only one thing at a time is necessary, so is it important to strive for change that is practical and feasible. You should not seek to reinvent yourself completely - the odds are that you are mostly good as you are - you just need to make some adjustments to the things that you are not pleased with. If you strive for 'good enough' in your habits you will have all the possibility to succeed. Strive for perfection and you'll set yourself up for failure. Giving up smoking cigarettes can be practical. It may not be practical to also never drink 3 liters of water daily, go to the gym five days a week, eat another candy bar and never scream at someone.

C – Clarity: Be Clear About What You Are Changing

Using what you have learned from monitoring to ensure that you are really specific about what areas of your habits you are improving and what your expectations are. This will be clearly evident for some habits - you want to give up smoking or throwing your clothes on the floor or biting your nails. For others, this may be less so – for example, some interpersonal habits like badgering, arguing or condemning may take additional information. Be very particular about what you want to be change, and what you want to do or say instead.

D – Date: Set A Date

Building in some anticipation is one way you can inspire yourself and get your energy levels up to combat this change of habit. Set a date for when you want to begin the change process, and begin to anticipate it. Let people around you know what you are going to do – that will make it more difficult to backtrack. Generate some anticipation about the date in yourself. That's the day you will actually begin a procedure that will make you feel very much better in the long run, even though it requires hard work to get going.

E – Elephants Never Forget

But you are not in any way an elephant! Look for ways to constantly remind yourself as to why this is happening. Think back to your list of pros and cons? Note down all of the primary motivations as to why you are attempting to alter your habit and pin the list somewhere you can regularly look at it. Pin it on the back of the door to your room, your computer monitor, your bathroom mirror or the fridge – a place where you will be able to see it multiple times a day. Consider writing down your target, and keep it as a reminder.

F – Falling Or Failing

You will be in a position to work out your habit 'danger times' with the help of your diary. You will have to be at alert at these times. Stay away from them if you can and if you cannot, shut down your "autopilot" - try as much as possible to be remain alert to be able to catch yourself before your habit kicks in. Attempt to identify the temptation to get involved in the habit before you start. When you feel the temptation, make a conscious effort to move on to something else.

We cannot often predict when the trigger will happen. If your habit typically happens when you are angry, you cannot see this coming at all. That being said, you can teach yourself to be more conscious that you might indulge in your habit when you are outraged, and be at alert against falling into it at those times.

G - Goodies

Have little ways in your strategy that you will reward yourself after every milestone is achieved. This could be with something nice to eat, (definitely not rewarding yourself with chocolate, if your aim is to lose weight!) a nice present to yourself (except if your goal is to spend less!), time spent playing video games or watching a movie, a warm shower – or something that will feel like a source of pleasure and that you'll look forward to doing. This does not have to be something extraordinary, but it is meant to be a gratification – not something that you do or will do every day. Be pleased with yourself but be careful about self-criticism. Do not tell yourself that your milestone is not an accomplishment because you should nevertheless be doing something morally correct.

H – Held Back: Watch Out For Negative Thoughts

Recall the thoughts we have established which may slow you down? Look out for your mind ambushing or setting traps for you as you go along with these. These may be as involuntary as the habits themselves. Telling yourself things like, 'I am never going to do this. It is too tough. I have always struggled before.' will not help you achieve your goal. Consider raising your awareness about these opinions. As soon as you find out that they are beginning to creep into your mind, get them out. Try visualizing yourself changing your habit instead. What will you feel or look like after changing that habit? Visualize the appealing, excellently-shaped nails you might have, or how your partner smiles when they notice your fragrance or aftershave, rather than the terrible smell of smoke.

I – Invite Support

Consider asking people around you to help you strengthen your efforts. Make an agreement with them in advance as to what they will (or will not) do. Maybe they can help you point out those bad habits when you do not know that you are doing them. Perhaps they can help with incentives after accomplishing a milestone. However, look out for issues here. It makes no sense to ask someone to help you point out your bad habits if you are going to lash out at them for helping out.

J – Juggle Things Around

Substitute bad habits with better habits. Find more tangible things to do with your hands other than scratching, picking or pulling with them. Eat something else or drink something else. It is far easier to replace a specific habit with another habit instead of doing nothing.

Dealing With Lapses Or Slip-Ups

Regardless of whether we are trying to break an old habits or create new ones, we rarely get it right at first. Lapses are unavoidable, and you need to understand that from the outset. If you have a lapse, it may be tempting to get angry with yourself or feel completely dispirited, and believe that you simply are not capable of doing the task. Both reactions can simply result into you giving up on everything. Try as much as possible to avoid this. You will be going back to square one if you decide to give up on everything. A lapse does not invalidate all that you have learned or accomplished – all of that still occurred. Remember what you have accomplished so far, even though it may seem very small, and start over. Ponder on what actually precipitated the lapse. Assess your feelings and thoughts about the setback and take lessons from them. How can this knowledge be incorporated into your new plan to reduce your chance of making a mistake again? Lapses are only an issue if you don't take lessons from them.

Chapter 6 - Dealing With Depression

Depressed is a word that we often use to define our mood when we feel miserable, somehow out of step or not at our best in the everyday language. That being said, it is somewhat different for those who suffer true depression. The way you perceive and interact with the world can be barely recognizable if you are depressed. Simple things makes you feel like you're ascending Mount Everest, even the smallest reverse of fortune can make you feel like it's the end of the world. The feeling of being depressed has been defined as "like wading through treacle" or like looking at the world via dark sunglasses, where colors turn shades of grey. Winston Churchill characterized his depression as being more like an extremely large dog which pursued him everywhere, pulling him down.

From time to time, everyone feels inferior or defective - it is totally natural. The way we experience a spectrum of emotions as a result of life events is doubtless part of what makes us human. It is something we all experience and usually only accept that we feel sad in reaction to disappointments, losses or just to have a 'bad day.' Broadly speaking, when we feel this way we can define roughly why we experience what we feel. The feeling normally passes relatively quickly, or when we do something to raise our spirit. Regular sadness should not be considered pathological in one way or another.

For some people, though, low mood remains with little to no respite for weeks, months or even years. This can be followed by other distressing symptoms like changes in sleep patterns, loss of appetite, tiredness, physical aches and pain or feelings of helplessness, alienation and worthlessness from people close to you. Studies have indicated that one out of every five persons will suffer depression. Depression also contributes to other challenging emotions, such as shame, embarrassment or anger.

Symptoms Of Depression

Do you recognize any of the following?

- Exhaustion, and fatigue

- Physical aches and pains

- Restlessness or anxiousness

- Feeling physically slowed down

- Prolonged depressed mood

- The thoughts of despair and worthlessness

- Concentration, memory and concentration difficulties

- Appetite changes - too little or too much food

- Changes in sleep patterns - too little or too much sleep

- Self-harm, or even suicidal thoughts

It is a pretty somber picture. There are some positive news in all that gloom though. We now accept depression and appreciate it much better than we did some few years ago. The stigma that surrounds this and other mental health issues is diminishing slowly. Many sufferers feel more comfortable to discuss what they have had to go through and share their challenges and coping techniques. A current 'Time to Change' initiative, emphasized the significance of overcoming the stigma associated with mental health issues such as depression. It utilized the stories of prominent celebrities like Ruby Wax, Alistair Campbell and Stephen Fry, proving that depression can happen to anybody. But the best news is that many tested and proven treatment options are now available that have benefited millions of people around the world. Those involve several types of medication, talk sessions, alternative and complementary therapies and group or social activities. Cognitive-behavioral therapy is one of the many available ways to help people with depression get better, and research proves it is one of the most successful.

When Does 'Normal' Low Mood Become Depression?

If you experience a complex and challenging event in life, such as death in the family or other loss, like redundancy, it would be abnormal not to experience any low moods. Such feelings may last a while, making it challenging to determine what should be considered 'normal' in a situation like this. Most the time, support and love from people close to you is what you need the most. Most of us recover from these kind of difficulties over time. But occurrences such as these can cause a more lasting and persistent depression for some people. Generally, if you have experienced physical and psychological signs of depression on many days, over several weeks, you are deemed depressed and may need support.

The following questions can help you know whether you are experiencing depression or not. Ponder about how you felt over the last 2 weeks. Did you encounter any of the following on a regular basis?

- Feeling really sad or irritated?

- Losing interest in things that you enjoyed in the past?

- You feel guilty or you feel terrible about yourself?

- Not being able to focus, recollect things or make choices?

- Any weight or appetite changes?

- Changes in pattern of sleep?

- Fatigue or energy-drenched feeling?

- A feeling of drowsiness or diminished activity that others have noticed?

- Do you feel like your circumstance is hopeless or you are completely useless?

- Death or suicide thoughts?

You may be depressed if you have experienced more than five of these symptoms for several days during the past two weeks. It is a really good idea to talk to your physician and explore the available treatment options if you think you are depressed. The self-help provided with the ideas proposed in this book may be an important part of treatment but should be performed with medical assistance.

Suicidal Thoughts Or Ideas

It might be disturbing if you or anyone close to you experience suicide or self-harm thoughts. We do not really talk about these things much, but they're much more prevalent than you might imagine. During challenging times, a large percentage of people might think that they should just sleep and not wake up, or that they were never be given birth to. There is a great deal of difference between having such thoughts and coming up with a plan to injure yourself.

It is a good sign that medical help is required if your thoughts begin to change into plans. Your hospital A&E department or your general practitioner are good starting points for help in the event of a crisis. Research has found that depression is directly related to chemical brain changes and makes it incredibly hard to think clearly, positively or in a healthy way. It is really crucial that we all seek support and assistance in times of crisis, and don't act on depressed thought process.

What Causes Depression?

Depression has no single cause. Some people say depression is as a result of "chemical disequilibrium" in the brain and scientific studies have proven that some brain chemicals change in people experiencing depressed mood. That being said, the root of depression for most individuals is a unique interplay between psychological (feeling and thinking), social factors (life) and biological (chemical).

Cognitive-behavioral therapy indicates that early experiences and life situations (like early losses, childhood traumatic experiences, bullying or bereavement) can make us more an easy target for depression later in life. That's because experiences like these lead us to establish fundamental negative opinions about ourselves, other people and how the universe works.

How CBT Can Help You To Tackle Depression Or Low Mood

Whether you are struggling with lifelong depression or just having a really bad day, the following recommendations can help you boost your mood. However, it is very important to consider asking for assistance if things are too much to be handled alone.

Step 1: Get Active

How would you score your present mood? On a spectrum numbered 0–10, where 0 is by no means low and 10 is by far the most depressed you've ever felt. All right, write it down. We don't want to do something when we're feeling really low. We almost always find it difficult to gather the strength to just get out of bed. However, if you obtained a score of 1 or more, here's the test: go out for a five-minute walk, right now. Yes,it doesn't matter if it's raining! It's just 5 minutes, so you're not going to freeze to death or drown!

Think of your posture when you walk. Keep your back straight and your head up. Look around. Pay attention to your surroundings including the people around you. What do you see? What do you hear and smell? Try as much as possible to make eye contact and smile at anybody you see, even if it does not sit well with you. If you're caught up with negative thoughts such as 'I can't do this' or 'I'm so fagged out' try to shift your attention back to the things going on around you. Walk quickly - faster than you want to move.

Rate your mood again after five minutes. So, how's it now? How would it be if you had spent these five minutes seated alone, languishing in your depressed mood? The possibilities are that your mood has gotten better a little or at least hasn't worsened, which is exactly what might have occurred if you didn't move.

Generally, we stop doing things that we usually take pleasure in when our mood is low because we do not want to do them. However, the less we do, the less we want to do. And therefore we feel worse. And so we still do less, feel even worse - and down the ferocious spiral we go.

This is a core principle of cognitive behavioral therapy for low mood. We have to take a look at our activity patterns and bring back things that we already stopped doing or are always avoiding. Sometimes that can require a lot of effort – we may no longer find pleasure in things that we usually enjoy and simple tasks may now require much more energy than before.

Step 2: Challenge Negative Thinking

Research has shown that thinking style changes when humans are depressed. Researches comparing depressed thinking with habitual thinking show that we tend to have a negative prejudice in how we assess the world when are depressed. We see adverse events and occurrences as our fault while dismissing positive outcomes or crediting others or chance with making them take place. When diagnosed with depression, it is as if we are putting on dark glasses and can only see darkness. Negative thoughts when you're depressed tend to be involuntary; we don't even know they are there. This is not really surprising given that the pessimistic essence of the thoughts is in complete sync with our low mood. Therefore, it blends together, and we are always unaware of the feelings, or in a position to question their precision. The very first thing that we are cognizant of, instead, is that we feel low. Stage one in addressing this is to get to know these feelings better. Next time you're feeling low, ask yourself 'what was running through your mind before you started feeling that way? If you begin to look, you'll find out that negative thoughts are there - you just need to be able to identify them.

Common Types Of Biased Thinking In Depression

There are several ways to distort our thinking style when we are in low mood. Let's discuss some of them now.

<u>Mental filter</u> - When we're small, we appear to note and highlight things that suit our negative perception of ourselves, other individuals, or the world as a whole. We forget about the fact that our manager has said that we had performed very well in another task or that we were honored last year for our excellence – we focus solely on issues that suit our negative perception, oblivious to something more stable or positive. Statements based on half the facts wouldn't hold water in court!

<u>Over-generalizing</u> - We show a tendency to make global statements about negative occurrences when we're depressed, making use of words like 'never' and 'always' in place of 'right now' and 'sometimes.' Be careful of these words. Then work on gathering all factual information, not just the negative. Try to understand that the way that things are now is really how they are. Things hardly ever remain the same, and we can't possibly foresee the future. Nothing is ever the same.

<u>Catastrophizing</u> - When we feel low, we almost always allow our thoughts to run into the worst possible outcome of a situation before anything truly happened. We conclude that such situations are bound to happen. Consider taking one issue at a time. The worst does not always occur, and catastrophes even lowers our mood. Alternatively, try thinking one thing at a time. You should take steps to avoid the very worst from happening. And surrounding yourself with catastrophes means you're more

likely to panic and less inclined to take meaningful action.

<u>Black and white thinking</u> - When we think of things as 'all or nothing,' it makes us feel unsatisfactory or grossly inadequate. The concern is that not so much is "all or nothing" in life. No one can be perfect and we'll never be happy if we still strive for perfection. Work towards doing a decent job, not perfection. Actually, work with the principle of "good enough is good enough" in trivial matters like washing the car.

<u>Mind-reading</u> - No matter how hard we try, we cannot actually read the thoughts of others – it would be much easier to become a psychologist if we could! We may be strong enough to read people, but we get our negative biases going when we are depressed. We have a tendency to presume that we know that people think negatively. Any thoughts as to why Rob didn't call? Perhaps he was preoccupied and he actually feels terrible for not having time to call, and he really likes you. Maybe Mum did think you looked sharp but was distracted, or just forgot to mention it. Don't jump to any conclusions that are based on partial assessments.

<u>Emotional reasoning</u> - The way we feel about something, sometimes, is not the ultimate guide to how it actually is. Try to look at the facts, rather than use your feelings as a manual. Ask others that aren't currently facing this emotional reaction what they believe. Assess the evidence individually from what it actually feels like.

Do you acknowledge or identify any of these biases in your thinking? They are very widely known ways to think when we are low in mood, obfuscate the way we see things, maintain, extend, and exacerbate depression.

Cognitive-behavioral therapy quite often gets criticized of being 'just about positive thinking. In reality, the way cognitive-behavioral therapy sees thoughts is that we should strive and reexamine them, not make them 'positive,' but instead find a more rational, healthy way of seeing and analyzing things. Any situation is rarely either all bad or all good. As Einstein wrote, 'the universe is the product of our thought; without changing our thinking, it cannot be modified.'

Silencing The Critic

Many of us use self-criticism as a source of motivation to spur us on. We may have learned over the years that being hard on ourselves can often inspire and motivate us to get us moving when we grow weak. That voice in your head saying 'come on lazy ass - you can't sleep all day long - get up and walk the dog or wash your mother's car. We are all acquainted with this, and can sometimes find it efficient in controlled amounts. The big issue is that when you're low, this voice in your head becomes a bully who will no longer worry about your best interests and is not inspiring, but assaulting. Since this bully is a piece of you, they know precisely what you are most angry and concerned about, and they can prey on some of these issues in a way that only further depresses you.

If you're trying to motivate a depressed friend to do well, which technique might work best?

You got this. You are more than capable of doing this. So you've made some bad decisions – that's normal. Pay attention to what you can do – I know you will get there if you just continue trying.

OR

You fool. How senseless are you? Take a look at all the wrong decisions you have made! You get it wrong all the time. Go on, try once more – give everyone a laugh.

Doesn't it seem evident? Even putting aside the fact that the second method is obviously unpleasant and insensitive, which of the two methods would probably be more productive in achieving the intended result? It seems quite clear that the first method is more empathetic and much more likely than the second to help somebody achieve what they're seeking to accomplish.

But when we condemn ourselves and beat ourselves within our own heads, we are applying the second method. No wonder we feel disappointed, frustrated and discouraged.

People who are efficacious in what they attempting to accomplish usually become their own best friend. They are reassuring, encouraging and sympathetic to themselves in the same way that we would want to be to a great friend.

Thinking About Thinking

Pay attention to your thoughts. How many thoughts do you think goes through your mind per day? How frequently do things that seem spontaneous and bizarre just pop up into your mind? Our minds are crowded, preoccupied and not every thought merits our attention. When we're stressed any bad thought that comes into our mind seems to catch our attention - we acknowledge it and conclude it's authentic just because it matches how we feel. It can sometimes take place without even being aware of it – negative thoughts accompany negative thoughts and our mental state tends to reduce. Teaching ourselves to become even more conscious of what is happening in our minds can reveal to us that thoughts are just thoughts - not truths. Thoughts can be tendentious, wrong and unenlightening, as we have seen. We can learn with practice to differentiate the good from the bad and decide which ones one to pay attention to.

Chapter 7 - Managing Panic Disorder With CBT

Agoraphobia panic disorder is a common and chronic condition characterized by severe declines in quality of life, the extreme use of general healthcare services, such as hospital emergency rooms and high economic and social costs. A main aspect of panic disorder is the recurrent experience of panic attacks - abrupt episodes of anxiety with disturbing physical symptoms including choking sensations, dizziness, shortness of breath, palpitations, heart racing, nausea or sweating. The fear many times is of dropping dead, loss of control, or going insane. The possible adverse consequences or results of such attacks remain the worry of patients with panic disorder. As a consequence, they almost always feel helpless in positions or circumstances that are difficult to walk away from, or where assistance cannot be easily accessible in the event of an unexpected need. Instances include crowds, public transportation, open spaces, elevators, unfamiliar or sparsely populated areas, bridges and highways with restricted access. If these circumstances are avoided or cause serious distress, the individual is said to have agoraphobia.

Cognitive-behavioral therapy (CBT) is an effective treatment for limited agoraphobia panic disorder. Standard CBT forms are usually administered over a span of several months across 10-12 sessions. If the agoraphobia is more intense, an exposure element is introduced, extending the duration of treatment.

An initial meta-analysis of clinical result studies for panic disorder with or without minimal agoraphobia showed that within the initial eight sessions the greatest progress was shown (Howard et al. 1986). Sokol and his colleagues subsequently found that after just a few sessions, panic attacks could be substantially reduced. Some workers have explored the possibilities to cut down the number of cognitive-behavioral therapy sessions or therapist interaction without substantial-effectiveness loss based on the findings. Both methods normally substitute therapist interaction with patient self-study materials, though the treatment time is generally 3 to 4 months. The findings of these experiments have been empowering. For instance, Clark et al. (1999) discovered that a five-session CBT versions coupled with the self-study modules were found to be on an equal footing with a standard 12-sessions treatment approach and advantageous to a waitlist control.

Patients with panic disorder with only mild agoraphobia were included in the preceding studies. There are few data accessible on the effectiveness of cognitive-behavioral therapy for patients with higher agoraphobia levels, but our clinical findings found that the effectiveness of agoraphobia increased, also when situational exposure guidelines were added. This inkling was supported by an early study involving PDA patients with moderate-to-severe agoraphobia in which it was discovered, based on individually constructed fear and preventative hierarchies, that the addition of gradient situation exposure instructions to standard cognitive-behavioral therapy did not significantly improve prevention. There was significant residual agoraphobic avoidance in both groups of patients (CBT with or without exposure guidelines) at post-treatment.

To resolve this problem, two top scientists together with some of their associates started a series of studies several years ago to create a more successful form of cognitive-behavioral therapy in panic disorder patients with mild-to-severe agoraphobia. The treatment described in this chapter is a result of this initiative and is an ongoing task. In creating it, I made great use of the above-cited work, along with the work of Feigenbaum and his associates at the Christoph Dornier Foundation in Germany. The emphasis on internal sensations as causes of anxiety and fear reactions is a significant aspect of this treatment. This is why I alluded to it as 'sensation-focused therapy' or 'sensation-focused intensive therapy' (S-FIT) when performed in its intensive way.

Treatment Overview

The procedure consists of three major components, defined in detail later: a short component of a largely self-study cognitive-behavioral therapy; an intense in vivo component for situational and interceptive exposure; and a relapse prevention and skill consolidation component. The exposure component comprises two days of therapist-supported, unrefined exposure and two or maybe more days of self-managed exposure. Therapist contacts are added to a patient workbook containing exercises and readings to be performed before treatment sessions. The first section of the workbook is sent to patients prior to commencing therapy.

The therapy is given in two arrangements. In one, patients are given treatment for a period of about three months in groups of 4-6 members. The cognitive-behavioral therapy component is issued across four weekly 1.5-hour group therapy sessions. Patients then work independently with a therapist for the two-day, therapist-supported part of the exposure component, after which they proceed to exercise self-managed exposure until the group reassembles. Once all the members finish the exposure component, they again come together for the relapse prevention and skill consolidation component for two more such bi- or tri-weekly 1.5-hour sessions.

In the second arrangement (S-FIT), a highly intensive treatment is provided to patients individually over an 8-day period. Patients are expected to spend full time on therapy during this period. As S-FIT is normally administered, the cognitive-behavioral therapy component is performed from Monday to Wednesday and requires three two-hour daily sessions. Exposure accompanied by the therapist takes place on Thursdays and Fridays. By Saturday, the patient acts without assistance by the therapist and continues the weekend's exposure practice alone. The component of relapse prevention and skill consolidation is delivered on Monday in a single two hours session. To date, the average therapist time per patient is 19 hours. This arrangement has been valuable to individuals living in an area where no PDA specialist is available or who have shagged out local treatment options; to people in immediate need of treatment (for example, at risk of losing their work opportunities or dropping out of college); and for individuals who want concentrated treatment. We will focus exclusively on the intensive treatment arrangement for the remainder of this chapter.

Features of Sensation-Focused Therapy for Panic Disorder

As previously stated, the current treatment symbolizes our effort, along with relapse-prevention approaches, to integrate active ingredients from established evidence-based procedures for panic and agoraphobia with a package that uses therapist time effectively. Consequently, several of the elements are comparable to other therapies. For example, cognitive restructuring is carried out just as it is done in standard cognitive-behavioral therapy. Symptom-induction therapies are carried out just as characterized in panic control therapy. Recent studies has shown that recurrent trials of mild panic provocation therapies (e.g., physical activity, intake of caffeine and hyperventilation) can result in reduced anxiety in some people with panic disorders. Additionally, the procedure consists of fundamental components of the exposure treatment pioneered by Fiegenbaum; i.e. cognitive exposure preparation, preceded by a decision period before exposure is started. However, the current therapy, particularly in its intensive form, varies in several respects from existing therapies.

First, this directly addresses the cognitive (fear of panic and associated feelings) and the behavioral (avoidance and protective behaviors) aspects of PDA. In comparison to other therapies which ideally concentrate on one or the other of these, the current therapy gives them approximately the same weight. It is achieved without substantially raising the treatment period by presenting the full content of the program within the self-study workbook that patients complete before appointments. Although there are companion patient workbooks for some established cognitive-behavioral therapy treatments, usually the books are used to strengthen and expand material conferred in a session. The treatment as implemented by the therapist is sufficient in itself. The opposite is true in the current treatment.

Second, the main focal point of therapy particularly during situational exposure, is on the fearsome somatic symptoms of anxiety and fear. As per this therapy, the objective is not to come to terms with agoraphobic conditions but rather to tackle the most terrifying internal feelings that can be induced. Agoraphobic circumstances provide such a valuable exposure context, but must be used together with aggressive symptom-induction treatments.

Third, patients are directed to experience terrifying sensations to the fullest and that includes full panic attacks. All behaviors that decrease the magnitude of sensations or the patient's consciousness or fear of them are regarded as counter-therapeutic. Whereas treatments to manage fear and associated somatic symptoms (e.g., relaxation or slow breathing techniques) or to use exposure manipulations, like graded sequencing of tasks to reduce discomfort, the standard approach emphasizes intentional agitation and full intensification of feared manifestations. Arousal mitigating techniques are not taught and their use is forbidden during treatment. In fact, whatever a patient does to relieve stress or feel better is removed completely (with the patient's active cooperation). Patients are also advised to welcome risks and unpredictability. For instance, the quest for triggers of panic attacks in order to make them more manageable or avoidable, as is prevalent in conventional cognitive-behavioral therapy, is de-emphasized in place of accentuating that all fear reactions (such as panic attacks), regardless of whether triggers are obvious or not, are basically the same.

The management of the ungraded mass exposure component often offers patients and therapists specific challenges. Current therapy makes every attempt to make the patients the top priority on the first exposure day, unlike traditional exposure therapies, where patients work slowly to improve their anxiety and avoidance hierarchies. Patients, and sometimes therapists, are overwhelmed by the strength of this research and the accompanying emotions. This calls for special skills on the side of the therapists, who really should gain knowledge on how to inspire patients to propel themselves to extreme ends and how to come to grips with refusal, dependency and anger with empathy. In the face of staggering fear, patients should learn to remain reasonable, to hold out against the powerful compulsion to escape and keep an eye on their feelings, thoughts and behaviors with scientific detachment. During this stage of therapy, therapists and patients may build strong emotions which must not be permitted to take the focus away from the objectives of therapy. If the therapist is too concerned about the obvious distress of the patient or retreats too easily, the patient will see this as a way of avoidance.

Particularly evident in S-FIT are the unique nature of the

therapeutic relationship. Many of the patients that have been treated in this format come from other countries and states at substantial emotional and financial costs. They have often made multiple unsuccessful treatment attempts and deemed this format their "last-ditch effort." If such patients significantly improve within a week, they on many occasions view the results as miraculous and the therapist as a magician. Termination for these patients may be harder than for people attended to with traditional therapies and special handling may be required.

Chapter 8 - Improving Your Sleep

Life can seem so much harder when we sleep poorly. Tiredness will make problems bigger and more daunting. Relationships can get complicated when we are irritable or frustrated, and everyday work and difficulties are much harder to resolve. If you're someone who has sleep issues, you're definitely not alone. Most of us have brief periods of sleeplessness when we are stressed, disturbed or under pressure.

How Can You Tell You Have A Sleep Problem?

Below is a simple way to see if you have a sleep disorder. Only answer YES or NO to the following questions:

Do you:

- Are you having trouble sleeping at night?

- Taking longer than half an hour to sleep?

- That your mind will not shut up and your thoughts will start to race through your head?

- Worry about everything and find that you can't turn off,

relax and sleep.

- Suffering from depression?

- Would have trouble going back to sleep if you are woken up by something?

- Usually wake up multiple times before morning?

- Wake up early regardless of how late you went to bed?

If you responded YES to three or more questions, you may be showing symptoms of insomnia. In the first place, it is often important to talk with your doctor about this situation, because sometimes there can be a medical trigger, which your physician can help you to cope with and to surmount. But let's say that you don't have something physically wrong and take it from here.

Cognitive-behavioral therapy will help you understand what causes a sleep problem. Many things can lead to a period of sleeplessness which, in most cases, lasts a few nights and then you have to do something that's different than normal.

The feelings, emotions, behavior and physical responses of people with ongoing sleep issues will, however, intervene to keep the trouble going. It eventually becomes a fatal loop - the more stressed we are about sleep, the less inclined we are to sleep. If we sleep throughout the day because we are exhausted, we will sleep less in the night again.

Case study - Robert

Robert's so troubled. He has always been a little worried and finds it particularly difficult when dealing with important work deadlines. This negatively impacts his sleep. Although he normally sleeps well enough and feels rejuvenated in the morning, but now he finds that it takes him several more hours to sleep. He lies awake and worries. He plays everything that could go poorly in his head if he does not reach his deadline. Scenarios becomes increasingly disturbing. Within 10 minutes of thinking he faltered to reach his deadline, was sacked, lost his career and he and his relatives are on the brink of starvation. 'This is far too horrendous for texts! I've to quit thinking this way! Robert take a look at his clock and it was 2 am! I have to wake up in exactly 5 hours ... I'll be so fagged out by tomorrow that I may never get anything done ... I have to sleep now! But I can't just get some.' And so now he begins to worry... and his worries starts all over again.

Case study - Simon

Simon was made redundant from his work recently. He fails to find a new job, which is counterproductive to his mood. Initially, he enjoyed his extra time by doing stuff around the house and meet friends, but now he finds it difficult to be inspired to do so. He avoids meeting people because he feels ashamed that he is unemployed and spends years sitting on his couch to watch television. During the day, he sometimes falls asleep on his sofa. He is lethargic and energy-drained. Often, after a few beers, he goes to sleep on the sofa late at night and goes really late to bed. He sleeps quickly, but then still wakes up often during the night. He often wakes around 3 or 4 a.m. and can't sleep again. He's sleepy and irritable throughout the day.

Both Simon and Robert have very common sleep problems. We will discuss how cognitive-behavioral therapy techniques can be used to support them later in this chapter. Let's talk about sleep and the patterns of sleep for now.

The most prevalent types of sleep disorder are:

- Poor quality sleep.

- Difficulty falling asleep

- Difficulty staying asleep

- Early waking

All this means that throughout the day, we feel physically and mentally drained.

There are clear proof that sleeping for one or two bad nights does not damage us much but makes us feel tired. Research indicates that people who have slept very little for one night can nevertheless perform tasks almost as efficiently as they usually did. This implies that a sleepless night, prior to an examination or interview, is doubtful to affect our performance significantly. We may not perform at our best, but we can still do things as usual.

Long disrupted sleep, however, can impair our concentration, our ability to effectively address problems or to make decisions. When people drive or run machines, it can be hazardous. It can also mean that we feel sad, anxious or irritable. And of course, these shifts in mood also influence both our jobs and our relationships.

The amount of sleep we have had is very difficult to determine accurately. When people have their sleep evaluated in a health center, they are often shocked that they actually sleep better than they imagined.

How Much Sleep Do We Need?

There is tremendous variability in how much sleep one person needs when compared to another person. Popular wisdom suggests 5 minutes more for the average citizen! However, the problem is 5 minutes more than what. At different points in our lives, our sleep requirements change. A baby sleeps on average for 17 hours a day. A child typically requires nine or ten hours a night, while the majority of adults need about eight hours. We are all different and unique. Many people require more than 8 hours, while others can require slightly less. We don't actually need less sleep later in life, but we adjust the type of sleep. Our sleep gets lighter as we grow older and wake more and more often. Contrary to the common opinion, it does not make a difference what period of the night we sleep, one hour before nighttime is the same as one hour after nighttime. However much sleep a person requires, it is crucial that our sleep helps us to feel renewed and ready to continue our lives during the day.

What Are The Different Stages Of Sleep?

The reason why we sleep is still a puzzle to us, even though scientists have several speculations about this. All animals sleep in a way that seems to provide our mind and body with some kind of restorative and reparative purpose. We know that when we sleep, we go through a variety of different phases. There are four major stages of sleep and during the night we can pass through them many times. We can wake more or less easily at various times. The stages involved are:

- Pre-sleep – Our muscles relax and breathe slow down as we switch between sleep and waking.

- Light sleep – When we are genuinely asleep but can still wake seamlessly.

- <u>Slow-wave or deep sleep</u> – The largest part of our sleep. We sleep deep and it's difficult to wake up. If woken, we can feel bewildered or disoriented. During this stage, we can sleep talk or walk.

- <u>REM (Rapid Eye Movement) sleep</u> – Even though our muscles continue to stay relaxed, our brains are actively engaged. Our eyes are moving quickly and we dream. REM's a fifth or so of our sleep.

A lot of people wake for a few seconds about every couple of hours. Usually we go back to sleep immediately and may not even know we've woken. Often these wakeful times will make us feel like we have slept less than we have.

Studies have proven that everyone dreams. However, some people recall their dreams more frequently. We don't completely comprehend the dream function. There is some scientific proof that if you dispossess someone of REM sleep, the next sleep will have a higher percentage of REM sleep. It seems like the body requires sleep such as this one, and if you lack it, your body will make up for it later.

What Can I Do To Help Myself Sleep Better?

Back in ancient times, opium was used by Greeks and Egyptians to sleep. Photos of Hypnos, Greek sleep god, typically demonstrate him holding a poppy flower. It is definitely not recommended today because we are much more conscious of the risks of the opium use and it is in reality a prohibited substance. Lettuce juice, alcohol, a plant called henbane and mandrake bark were also used in ancient times as sleeping aids. Although we obviously recommend none, don't despair because you can do a lot to enhance your sleep.

The following strategies and improvements will fix the issue for most people with sleep disturbance. However, adjustments to your sleep will lead to changes in bad habits so your body and mind will learn how to sleep efficiently for several years to come. In other words, it can be difficult to adjust your sleep pattern and routine and require time and effort. It is critical that our advice is followed regularly and over a duration of time. This advice sometimes sounds too simplistic and people argue that all the ideas have already been tried. However, the methods were often used inconsistently and only for one or two nights at a time. It can be difficult to stick to new habits, but if you will persevere, you can see significant improvements in the sleep quality.

These recommendations won't work for everyone, so you might need to try it out to see what feels right for you.

Step 1: Monitor Your Sleep

<u>Keep a sleep diary</u>. As we said, it can be difficult to predict how much sleep we get. A diary will help you to determine your sleep habits and problems. This will help you recognize the adjustments that you need to implement and where you need to begin. Hold your diary for a while before you talk about what you gained from it. Then consider the methods and approaches suggested in the next steps. Which of these appear to match with the issues your diary highlights?

Step 2: Adjust Your Environment

<u>Look at your sleeping environment</u>. Do you have the right temperature to sleep safely? Is it too bright or maybe too dark? Is there something you can do to decrease the noise? Is your bed safe and comfortable? Everyone is unique and so finding the right sleeping setup may require the try and error process. You have to be very comfortable in bed. It might be worth investing in a new bed or even a more comfortable mattress.

<u>Consider your partner</u>. You can have additional issues if you don't sleep alone. Many partners find that they have separate night rest requirements. Maybe one partner snores or sleeps very restlessly. Maybe each likes a different form of mattress. Considerations like these may require some dialogue and

negotiation. Some couples find that sleeping apart will work for them, as long as they are clear why it is important. This approach certainly doesn't mean you avoid sharing a bed – only that one or the other retires to another bed when you want to sleep.

Step 3: Change Your Sleeping Behavior And Habits

Develop a bed-time routine. Around an hour and a half before bed, begin to send your body signs that it is time to sleep. You might try a warm shower, a hot cup of tea, listen to calming music or watch or read something calming. It is essential that your brain at this time is not overstimulated. Don't do any work, workout aggressively, or read or watch something very enthralling within two hours of you going to bed.

<u>Watch what you eat and drink</u>. Caffeine from beverages including coffee, tea and coca-cola is a stimulant and can remain in your body for a long period of time. Stay away from them for hours before going to bed. Additionally, consuming too much in the evening may imply that you have to go to the restroom in the night. Seek to drink much of the liquid that you really need earlier in the day. Don't eat a big meal within few hours of going to bed, but do not go hungry to bed. It's also beneficial to eat a relatively balanced diet.

<u>Cut down on alcohol and tobacco</u>. Alcohol can help you sleep,

and within a few hours you are more likely to wake up and then find it almost impossible to sleep again. Stop any alcohol drink few hours before going to sleep. Tobacco is a stimulant which can mess with the capacity of your body to rest. Again, stop smoking just before going to bed.

Be strict about bedtime. When you try to boost your sleep, make sure you go to bed always and wake up every day at the same time. Choose a bedtime when you will usually start to feel tired. It might be 10 p.m. for some, or about 1 a.m. for others. Build a routine that gives you about 8 hours in bed. The main thing is that you wake up at the time you planned for yourself, even if you have slept poorly and feel broken. A very noisy, repeating, unreachable alarm clock can help. Don't nap in the afternoon. Wait till when your set bedtime has reached. Once you have successfully established schedule and are sleeping much better, the odd late morning or night will not negatively impact you, but try to keep to a good routine as much as possible. If you can adhere to a consistent schedule, your body will actually have a normal rhythm and you can sleep a lot better. This can be very frustrating for the first few days and during the day it can be frustrating to avoid napping. It will help to enlist the assistance of people around you to motivate you to sustain it.

Don't lie in bed not sleeping. If you do not sleep in 15 minutes after heading to bed, get up and go do something else, preferably in another room. This helps you break the cycle of making things worse by not stressing about not feeling sleepy. When you're tired, go back to bed. Repeat it after 15 minutes if you can't sleep again. You will have to get up at your set time whether you were able to sleep or not.

Associate your bedroom with sleep. If you normally read, work or think in bed, this can imply that when you go to sleep you are not comfortable. Move this thinking out of the bedroom. Your mattress should be only reserved for sleep and sex. Read only when you know that it relaxes and makes you sleep. Take into account what you've been doing reading. Is it likely that your mind will become relaxed or stimulated? Bridging these patterns would ensure that when you go to bed, you prompt your mind into sleep.

Use relaxation techniques. Seek self-hypnosis, deep relaxation and several other methods of relaxation. Some of them are probably simpler and more fun than you might have thought. Understand that it is typically easier to learn to use these techniques during the day before you can start using them to help you sleep. When you've found a good technique, you can use it to calm down and ready your mind and body for sleep.

Increase physical exercise during the day. We all sleep much better when we get busy and expel energy during the day. Aim to increase your level of physical activity. If this isn't for you, you don't have to go to the fitness center or take up a sport. Think of your trip to your workplace or shopping trip. Can you park your car farther away from where you are heading, instead of orbiting to find the nearest place? Could you get off trains and buses a stop earlier or later than your regular one and get a bit of a trek? A quick 20-minute walk can be an excellent workout and can change your pattern of sleep. However, ensure you have this workout earlier in the day and not two hours before bedtime.

<u>Increase enjoyable and calming exercises during the day and night</u>. Most of us work really hard these days and find little time to do things we like or help us relax. It can impact our mood, make us nervous and make sleeping very difficult. Strive to do something you enjoy daily, no matter how small. Think in an innovative way. It does not have to be something huge. Learning for fun, playing a game or even walking around the garden might all you need to feel more relaxed. We are much more likely to sleep better if our mood is better.

Step 4: Manage Your Unhelpful Thinking

Negative thoughts about sleep and general problems may lead to agitation, anxiety or stress, enhanced muscle tension or less positive behavior. All this stops us from sleeping well. To improve the way we sleep, we have to change our way of thinking and act with respect to our thoughts.

<u>Deal with low mood or anxiety</u>. Mood disorders like panic

attack, anxiety or depression can lead to sleep problems. The chapters in this book will help you find solutions to solve these issues. Using our questionnaires to find out what the challenge might be. It may be a symptom of depression to wake up very early in the morning and not be able to get back to sleep. Speak to your doctor about getting more support if you are worried that you might be seriously depressed or anxious.

<u>Reduce worry</u>. We have already discussed how many consider it disturbing that lying awake keeps them from sleeping. You can support yourself by making yourself aware when you slip into a cycle of worry and make it very clear to yourself that this is not the period to feel worried. If you often get worried in the morning, set a fixed amount of time during your bedtime routine as 'worrying time,' when you allow yourself the chance - and indeed approval - to ponder about all these things that might worry your mind. Seek to write it down and address the things you can resolve before you go to bed. Once you've had time to worry about the night, keep your mind firm if your worries try to start again. Concentrate and focus entirely on something more fun and stimulating, like a childhood memory, planning a holiday trip or simply counting digits in your head. Keep in mind that what you focus on spreads, and it will help you shut off not wake up. If you're worried you're going to forget things, keep a paper and pen near your bed. Write down things, and after that move on to something else. Remember that you're not going to forget them, it's all written on paper already, and

that's not presently your time of worry - you have to wait for tomorrow's slot.

<u>Tackle worry about not sleeping</u>. If you lay awake and think 'I can never get to work effectively tomorrow if I don't sleep,' you will find it more difficult to shut off and rest. This can become a continuous cycle, as seen in the chapter above. You may have to work to break this loop. Remember that while you will be tired, your performance will not immediately be affected. Part of sleeping is enabling your body to rest physically so consider making this your main objective instead of sleep. Relax the muscles and focus on calming thoughts. Move your alarm clock away from your bed so that you don't have to keep looking at the time.

Nightmares

Nightmares can be really disturbing. Some people can be scared to get back to sleep if they have one. There are also some hypotheses as to why some of us have nightmares, while others do not. It is widely accepted that we are more likely to have nightmares when we are outraged, frightened or depressed. If you wake up from a terrible dream, you first have to remember that it really was just a dream, and that your mind only works out things by itself. Writing the dream will also reduce the grip it has on you. It can be a way to make it feel smaller and less important if you see it on paper, strange and meaningless. You can just take a peculiar look at the strange things in your mind, without giving them any additional nefarious meanings.

Should I Use Sleep Medication?

Your doctor may prescribe different medicines to help you sleep. Over time, some of the medicines may become addictive and leave you feeling exhausted and sober the next day. The body will get used to it over time, which means you need higher doses. The same can be valid of medicines that you can purchase without prescription over the counter. Sleep medications generally can only be used to treat acute sleep disorders in the short term, when for instance someone is so depressed that they cannot find sleep at all, every night.

There are also herbal treatments available that are beneficial to certain people. However, you should develop better routines and behaviors to help you sleep naturally instead of relying on some kind of medication to help you sleep.

Chapter 9 - Coping With Bad Times

What does cognitive behavioral therapy say about cases in which our so-called negative thinking may be right? Maybe you lost somebody you love. It could be true to say, "I will never get to see that man again." It's not overblown or other kind of negative manipulation – anybody, unsurprisingly, would be exceedingly troubled. We all sometimes experience painfulness in our lives, but some people are facing tougher things than others.

Here are some occurrences that have proven to be presumably the most challenging in Western society. Have you in one way or the other experienced any of them?

- Prison penalty.

- Period of housing problems or homelessness.

- The death of a parent, spouse or even other close member of the family.

- Significant debt or financial troubles.

- A close friend's death.

- Divorce or breakup of a family.

- Breakdown of a relationship.

- Unwanted pregnancy or stillbirth.

- Unemployment.

- Severe illness of yourself or a family member.

If you have ever experiences one or more of what is on that list, evidence shows that both physical and mental health conditions are more likely to come up, and you may find yourself less equipped to deal socially. The more experienced you have, the worse you will feel.

Obviously, it's not quite as straightforward and easy as this. A person's responses to stress are determined by several variables. Some individuals are more resilient and thus better able than others to deal with stressful events. While some variables such as biological vulnerabilities, educational or cultural events are far beyond our influence, we can do many things to boost our chances of dealing with stressful events more effectively. Unlike common perception, some people are not only stronger than others. Our endurance and ability to withstand stress varies throughout our lives, and people known to be "solid" may feel submerged at times by issues they dealt with effectively at other times.

It is beneficial to think that we all have limited capability for stress, rather like a bucket that can hold a finite quantity of water. We all feel a certain amount of stress in our daily lives. In reality, some stress is required to inspire and encourage us to act. However, if our stress bucket is constantly almost full, it will not take much more to spill over or for us to develop difficulties in coping. And that is why sometimes an apparently simple problem coming on top of many other relatively simple problems finally makes us feel like we are going to collapse. Perhaps we managed to cope with everything effectively until then, but this is where it all comes to an end with tears.

Studies have shown that several factors determine how negative life circumstances, big or small, impact us. Some of these will be briefly explained in a moment. Peruse each one and reflect on your own personal experiences. How have they armed you to deal with stressful life situations? Are there certain ways in which you are susceptible to stress, or in which you are more irrepressible? Negative experiences can on many/numerous occasions work in various ways at different times for different people. Often we can learn from situations and become stronger by learning from those experiences. At some other times we may not be able to cope and the roughly similar negative experiences can have a much stronger impact. If you are unable to deal with stress effectively, there are likely many legitimate reasons for this. It definitely not because you're just feeble.

Key factors determining coping:

- Historical factors

- Personality traits

- Meaning of the event

- Identification of your strengths and abilities

Let's take a closer look at these. The connotation that we give to events will affect our responses and our ability to deal with them. For instance, if we believe that we have caused an issue by doing something inaccurate, our reaction depends on if we understand our mistake or not. When we acknowledge that the error is forgivable, we will be able to learn from it and make positive changes against another time. But if we think that we are 'evil' or deficient, we may feel powerless to improve and learn from the event. One way of thinking means that we can all feel good about ourselves and any other way of doing things does not.

If we assume that we have the skills and capacities to cope and handle a situation, however bad it may be, then we will use methods more likely to produce a successful result. There are approach-related techniques such as problem-solving, learning from challenging situations and using other people's support.

But we are less likely to use approaches if we feel we cannot deal with it or that the problem cannot be fully handled. The methods of avoidance include trying to stay away from others, minimizing activities we usually do, using alcohol or drugs to get away or pretending that the issue is not there and fruitlessly hoping that it will eventually vanish. Unsurprisingly, these methods have been proven to be less efficient.

Also important for coping with stress are historical factors including upbringing, education and early life experiences. If we have been informed that showing emotion imply that we are soft, we may be upset at the usual reactions under the situations. And, for example, if we lose a close partner or friend, we may do less well than admonish ourselves to experience very natural feelings like sorrow and sadness. But it will be easier to handle and we can better manage it if we have been taught that we can communicate and express emotions, even though our sadness will still be so intense.

Personality traits like sociability or optimism can make us more or less prone to stress. Social reinforcement has been proven to be very essential in our way of handling issues after a stressful life situation. Therefore, there is an advantage for those who are inherently sociable or form friendly connections.

Many other components play a role in how well you deal with situations. These components or factors include your age, socio-economic reputation or stage of life. Some of the mentioned factors are obviously more within our influence than others. The interpretation you give to happenings and your prognostication of how you'll respond are fundamental to cognitive-behavioral therapy. When you finish the book, you will probably have learned to recognize and deal with them in very various ways.

The great news is that none of these are impossible to overcome in terms of the impact of historical influences and personality traits. Regardless of the situation, all of us can better manage stress, regardless of upbringing, sex, age or experience.

Golden Rules For Coping With Stressful Life Events

In this section, we are going take a look at the guiding principles for coping with a difficult situation and taking care of yourself during a rough time.

1. Take Care Of The Basics

It's enticing to curl into a ball under the blanket when terrible things happen and get out of the everyday activities and behaviors. Taking care of your essential necessities is Meeting your essential necessities is much more relevant at this moment. You may not feel like eating anything, and sleeping seems somewhat difficult, but you caring for yourself is important. Eat small meals instead of attempting to force down regular meals – stressful periods can sap our energy and our bodies require food, even though our mind is insisting that we're not starving and do not want the food. Try to relax as much as possible even if your sleep is interrupted. A lot of people think responsible use of sleeping tablet can be beneficial to get you through the first few nights after something complex and challenging has occurred.

2. Keep (Reasonably) Busy

Going through our normal daily movements can be very helpful in tough times. If you normally take your dog for a morning walk or run out for an afternoon paper at the local store, try to maintain these practices. We all have intimate activities that can help us remain in contact with everyday life, and we do nearly on autopilot. In tough times, they can prove calming, and can also encourage us that our life is still moving on and that we can still influence at least some parts of it. Sometimes we have to pass through the movements in order to be able to survive. Please take note - people sometimes use work or other things to conceal or suppress emotions. This can make their recovery to take longer.

3. Exercise

This might be the last thing you feel like taking part in. There is however good proof that regular exercise is essential for low mood and stress management. Even a short stroll around the block or in a park will still boost your mood and hopefully make you feel more optimistic than just sitting and dwelling on your troubles. Get moving! Go on, push yourself to do physical activities - even if it is only for five minutes.

4. Allow yourself to feel sad

This may sound a bit odd, but a lot of people spend too much time battling their normal and natural reactions to what has actually happened to them. Failures and setbacks can bring grief. Feeling and voicing pain and grief is neither feeble nor meaningless. It can actually be the only way to heal and move forward. Everybody experiences and conveys emotions distinctively.There is no wrong or right way to doing it. However, we only make it worse when we battle and struggle against feelings of pain.

Think about what you can do if you got caught up in a quicksand. Your first instant reaction would be to fight hysterically to break free. But that's just the exact reverse of what you are suppose to do. The more you float around, the quicker the sand will pull you under. Your safest choice is to stop fighting, to lie down flat and gently inch forward. The same rule applies to painful emotions. Stop fighting and try to endure pain. Just stay with it. Don't combat the emotions – they're going to get stronger and try to pull you down. Try to remind yourself that what you are experiencing is normal, natural and comprehensible. Above all, remember that you will recover with time and feelings will go away. This doesn't mean your loss will be completely forgotten or eradicated, but your emotions will be less painful and less distressing over time. Some issues will still hurt, but slowly they will have a reduced impact on your ability to perform - even though it seems difficult or a long way off when you're going through it.

Just get yourself to feel that way when you're sad.

Remember:

- There's a reason you feel this way.

- That is exactly how you are feeling right now.

- There are going to be good days and bad days.

- Emotions change and even sorrow comes and goes in magnitude.

- Enjoy the most of the good days and be good to yourself on the bad days.

- Do things that will assuage you and encourage you, and be patient with yourself.

- Attend to yourself the same way you would attend to a close friend or a child in distress.

- When you show yourself compassion you will recover quicker.

- Don't reprimand yourself or say things like "you need to be over it by now."

- Be your own best friend.

- Do that which is good for you.

It's absolutely pointless telling yourself to 'pull yourself together'. If it were that straightforward, you would have done it long ago and there won't be a need for this book.

5. Watch Out For Distorted Thinking

I mentioned at the beginning of this chapter how some negative thoughts are unavoidable at tough times in our lives, and might even be completely accurate. But it does not mean all of them are. There are times like this where we can still have inaccuracies and misinterpretations in our reasoning. Pay attention to the things that are going through your mind. How correct are the judgments that you make and the stuffs that you say to yourself? How beneficial are all these to you?

Have you ever realized how it can be extremely difficult, if not unthinkable, to see the stars in the night sky of a city? This is because we are prevented from seeing the brightness of these stars by the light pollution caused by towers, streetlights and automobiles. The beautiful thing is that these stars are still and will always be there. We are just unable to see them. As soon as we turn off the lights or travel to the countryside we will be able to see the stars again. It is somewhat like this with wonderful things in our lives when we are in distress. We can't see anything good but reminding ourselves that they are still there within us is so necessary. When our condition improves and the painful feelings fade even a little, then the good starts to emerge and becomes visible again. None of this is about disregarding the negatives or avoiding them. They all are too genuine. It's about realizing nothing is ever pure black or pure white.

6. Cut Down On Self-Criticism

It's not likely to be beneficial if you call yourself weak just because you are "not coping" at the moment. Recognize this? Be your own best friend. You should be solid and motivate yourself to push forward - but at the right momentum and in a caring, compassionate way. You will discover that this is far more impactful than worrying yourself to respond in a very regular manner, which you would likely easily understand and forgive in other people.

7. Lean On Others

In challenging times, we all need support and assistance. It can be very difficult to accept that we need assistance or are not rising to occasion as much as we'd we like. This can make us feel vulnerable or worthless, and that people whose views we hold in high esteem think less of us. But we can also be pleasingly amazed when we take the first step to seek assistance. In general, a lot of people are happy to offer assistance. We all like to be wanted or to feel supportive which can also make us feel good about our own lives. Give the individuals around you a chance. Reach out and seek for assistance – even if it is in small ways. You'll likely be astonished with the results. Be smart in your decisions – only approach those that you think will be happy to support you and let them know the things that you need. If you can be courageous enough to share your needs and desires, chances are that these needs will be fulfilled. If assistance is not provided, try to let go of any frustration that you may feel – you have more than enough to deal with already.

8. Write It Down

There are reports that writing about traumatic events can make people feel more optimistic and can also minimize the amount of traumatic ailments they endured in the months following a stressful event.

When Do Usual Responses To Stress Become A Mental Health Condition?

It's a fact that traumatic life experiences can often cause mental health issues like anxiety or depression. Professionals find it very difficult to tell exactly where 'normal' responses end and issues with mental health starts. It takes some time for some players to adapt or adjust to an traumatic life event or loss – it may take months or even years feel comfortable or be able to move on with your life altogether. In cognitive-behavioral therapy, people are advised not to undergo active or formal therapy in the first few months following a traumatic life event because challenges like depression and anxiety are normal response to an abnormal occurrence in a person's life. That being said, it can as well be possible that some people for some reason get trapped after a traumatic life event and find it almost impossible to move on and reconstruct their lives.

If you think something like this has happened to you, the first thing you should do is to genuinely ask yourself if you're not demanding too much of yourself. Sincerely, is it reasonable to assume to be 'over it' by now? If you feel that you may be anxious or depressed, then speak about it with people around you. Do they also believe that you are depressed? The people around you can sometimes be able to evaluate this much better than you. Most pertinently, if you think that the situation is getting out of control and the self-help techniques recommended in this book aren't working, even after putting in all your time and effort, then seek for assistance. What's the opinion of your GP?

Post-Traumatic Stress Disorder (PTSD)

I've spoken about very normal, yet complicated, and stressful life events in this chapter. However, the traumatic incidents we are looking at in this segment are in a different class. The type of events that could lead to the development of PTSD are the ones people acknowledge to be very dangerous and life-threatening either to them or to the people around them, and they are powerless to do something about it. Although uncommon, traumatic events can happen to anybody. Reading media stories will make you wonder how people have to live with circumstances like serious injury or death. PTSD occurs when typical reactions to traumatic events:

- Start within six months of the incident or trauma period.

- Continue after this period for more than 3 months.

- Begin over 6 months after the trauma event – this is termed PTSD delayed-onset.

Individuals with traumatic events experience extreme terror, powerlessness or panic. Traumatic incidents that are outside our normal knowledge. Therefore, divorce, job loss, bereavements (with the exception of those triggered by traumatic events), chronic disease, and marital or domestic dispute do not count as trauma even though, as we have shown, they may potentially cause severe stress and even depression and anxiety. PTSD has a very unique set of symptoms, separate from mental health conditions, although PTSD patients can as well experience some symptoms of both anxiety and depression. Common examples of traumas that may contribute to PTSD include combat situations, attacks or assaults, road traffic accidents, and being trapped in natural catastrophes or terror attacks.

Typically, after a traumatic incident, a lot of people experience some of the below reactions:

- Distressing feelings, memories, pictures, dreams or repeated trauma flashbacks – often, there are blank parts that the person cannot remember.

- Avoidance; you try to avoid activities, conversations, thoughts, places, people, feelings, or anything that might stimulate trauma memories or thoughts.

- Emotional tiredness, detachment, difficulty or inability to develop loving feelings.

- Seeing the future as directionless, meaningless, and probably short-lived.

- Losing confidence and avoiding things you've once enjoyed doing.

- Enhanced arousal – you're easily frightened and don't like sudden noise or bright light.

- Sleeping problems, irritability, frustration, concentration difficulty, increased vigilance.

These reactions can at first be very natural and almost always pass after some time or after following some effective coping strategies. For some people, however, and for reasons we don't yet actually understand, these side effects don't go away and may even become worse over time. Have you witnessed a traumatic incident and all of the above reactions? If they don't pass away or worsen over time, you will find some useful exercises later in this chapter. But after following the exercises and things still don't get better, or even gets worse, then it's very necessary to seek support from your doctor or a licensed mental health professional.

Why Do Flashbacks Happen?

I don't exactly understand why the brain relives things like it does following a traumatic event. However, psychologists think this is linked to the way the brain processes occurrences and retains them as memories. Just assume your memory is very much like the linen closet of a tidy, coordinated housewife (or fiancé). Each material is first organized, folded neatly, and then set aside in an arranged manner. Bedsheets go with bedsheets in one stack, and duvet covers are all also together in another stack. Our memories are trapped inside when the door is shut. When something takes place and we decide to open the door, we can take out a memory and evaluate it or use it. Sometimes things fall out of the shelf at odd or wrong times, but we can pack things up again, and this isn't a big deal.

Now imagine that a huge, oddly shaped duvet comes along and must be placed in the closet. It does not fit and will not fold into a nice, arranged form and regardless of how much you try force it in, it just keep falling out and forcing the door to open. This is exactly what seems to take place with traumatic memories. At first, it does seem to our brains that such memories cannot be understood or properly handled, possibly because they are so far out our normal life experiences and expectations. There's no framework to fit them in. It is as if our brains still have to re-experience the memory and try to interpret it – before packing it away. We just don't remember it in the ordinary way, but as a fresh event – just as if it's currently happening now – not as a regular memory from the past. There is proof that the part of the brain that is linked to traumatic memories is the same part that we have discussed when looking at anxiety, connecting with our flight or fight mechanism. Each time this event comes into our minds, all of our anxiety reactions are triggered. Flashbacks may be terrifying and awful, but they might also be the way our brain seeks to heal itself. Luckily, there are ways of helping your brain to achieve this.

What You Should Do

Let yourself embrace the entire variety of emotions you are experiencing. Remember that these are totally normal under the situations. They don't imply that you're 'going insane,' 'being miserable,' or you're doing any similarly meaningless name-calling.

Now take a look at what you have been doing differently before the traumatic event. Are you being excessively cautious? If you were ambushed, are you now reluctant to leave your residence after dark, even though you are living in a safe neighborhood? If what you're doing is really being over-cautious, particularly in comparison to before, make a list of all the things you're avoiding now and begin to face them one at a time, maybe you should try by starting with the easiest. You could even ask a family member or friend to accompany you, but then move on to doing it alone if no one is available to help, just as you've done before. It can be very scary at first, but as you reiterate the actions and find that nothing terrible is happening, you will likely find your self-confidence growing slowly.

It's so necessary that you reassess the actual event, maybe by discussing it with someone. Perhaps something really needs to be learned there. You may decide to install a burglar alarm in the case of a violent burglary and use it for some rooms even while you are in the building. If you've experienced a car accident that was related to driving in bad weather, you might want to take an advanced driving course. Focus on distinguishing between what is a rational, more careful response, from the potentially very drastic course of action being determined by your fear alone.

Conclusion

Cognitive-behavioral therapy reflects an alignment of the cognitive, behavioral and other ideologies of human conduct and psychopathology (that is, developmental, social). The various techniques of cognitive-behavioral therapy reflect its dynamic and integrative past, including problem-solving, conditioning, cognitive restructuring, modeling, and development of personal coping techniques, mastery, and self-control. Cognitive-behavioral therapy addresses several potentially vulnerable areas (e.g., cognitive, behavioral, or affective) and offers opportunities for intervention. Cognitive-behavioral therapy is also viewed as the best therapy for mental health problems in young people. Further work is needed to understand the outcome of treatment mediators, moderators, and predictors, and to pursue the promulgation of effective cognitive-behavioral therapy approaches.

The importance of using cognitive behavioral therapy in the treatment of mental health issues is indisputable because it teaches a person who is frequently wary of CBT's beneficial outcomes, the negative consequences of his or her own self-defeating thought processes and maladaptive behavior. Aaron Beck first used this form of method to overcome the helplessness and depression he experienced. The book explores what cognitive-behavioral therapy is, including several specific cognitive-behavioral therapy techniques that contribute to the essential factors behind the treatment's beneficial impact on individuals with psychological problems, first by addressing the cognitive side and then the therapy's behavioral component.

Cognitive-behavioral therapy is a method that incorporates the cognitive therapy and behavioral therapy approaches into one treatment. Cognitive therapy teaches the client how patterns of thinking influence their emotional state and behavior. Cognitive therapy enables the patient to change patterns of unreasonable and negative thinking to ease the emotional distress caused by these thoughts. Behavioral therapy educates the client on how to change a reactions that trigger escape, avoidance, and anxiety of particular situations.

It is a commonly held belief that our thoughts actually influences our emotions and actions, not external stimuli, and the cognitive component of cognitive-behavioral therapy is based on the emotions of the patient. There are a number of different ways of understanding any given stimulus. Many explanations are undoubtedly more logical than others, or more encouraging. The patient recognizes negative and irrational thoughts through exercises in thought analysis and starts to replace them with more logical and constructive thoughts. Automatic thoughts are by far the most effective in influencing our emotions and behaviors, as they are the cognitive responses to situations that are feared. Automatic thoughts creates expectations and has an impact on core beliefs. Cognitive-behavioral therapy targets negative and delusional beliefs and thoughts in the patient's mind.

Cognitive-behavioral therapy is built on Socrates' assertion that logical reasoning is based on reality, not inference. This is the unfounded negative beliefs, which are seldom true, that have such detrimental impact on people as they are so disturbing to the person's psychological well-being. Generally, clients don't grasp the negative consequences of their own thought. Cognitive-behavioral therapy therapists work with patients to teach them how their thought habits influence their psychological conditions and behavior.

People who undergo cognitive-behavioral therapy still feel very skeptical about the treatment. The patient sometimes feel they can't adjust the way they think because it's just a fundamental part of who they are. The patient discovers the importance of these thoughts and their effect on behavior by analyzing irrational and negative thoughts. The patient learns to search for truth that can be verified by more reliable proof gathered. Cognitive-behavioral therapy helps the patient to reduce his/her negative and irrational thought by exposing the individual to logical and realistic analysis.

The behavioral side of the treatment recognizes the patient's major behavioral problems, which primarily manifest as avoidance and escape from some life circumstances, and seeks to alter this maladaptive behavior. The therapist gives the client valuable knowledge about the harmful consequences of the destructive patterns of behavior. Because of an unreasonable fear or phobia linked to a particular situation, the client can avoid certain situations. By avoiding or escaping such situations, the client generates more fear of them as this fear builds within the patient's mind with every avoiding or escaping acts. The behavioral therapy process gradually teaches the client to tackle those situations that would usually be overlooked. The patient starts to become used to them by constantly witnessing previously avoided or prevented situations and begins to understand that his or her previous concerns regarding these given situations were unfounded. Therefore, the patient starts to lower the number of automatic avoidance and escape circumstances and can halt the vicious cycle with a more rational approach to things.

Cognitive-behavioral therapy has a massive impact on psychologically disordered patients. The benefits of this therapy have been shown to be highly effective in coping with many psychological disorders by overcoming irrational and even negative unconscious thinking and modifying behavioral responses to circumstances, causing anxiety and avoidance. Specific cognitive-behavioral therapy methods involve evaluating one's unconscious thoughts and replacing them with more logical and constructive alternative thoughts based more on reality and slowly revealing and accustoming the individual to circumstances that are feared. Positive effects of cognitive-behavioral therapy come from attacking and defeating thoughts and behaviors that can trigger negative emotions. Cognitive-behavioral therapy is important as it educates the patient about the negative connotation of the maladaptive thought patterns and maladaptive conduct that has been engendered in the individual and directs the client to base his reasoning on evidence rather than assumptions. This, in effect, has the most important impact on the stable and constructive course of the patient's behavior.